KATE MOSS

THE MAKING OF AN ICON

CHRISTIAN SALMON

HARPER
DESIGN
An Imprint of HarperCollinsPublishers

ALSO BY CHRISTIAN SALMON

▬▬▬▬▬

Tombeau de la fiction, Denoël, Paris, 1999

Censure! Censure!, Stock, Paris, 2000

Devenir minoritaire. Pour une politique de la litérature, Denoël, Paris, 2003

Verbicide. Du bon usage des cerveaux humains disponibles, Climats, Castelnau-le-Lez, 2005 (reprinted by Actes Sud, "Babel" collection, Arles, 2007)

Storytelling: La machine à fabriquer des histoires et à formater les esprits, Éditions La Découverte, Paris, 2007 (reprinted by La Découverte/poches, 2008)

Storytelling: Bewitching the Modern Mind. Verso Books, New York: 2010.

Storytelling Saison I: Chroniques du monde contemporain, –Les Prairies Ordinaires, Paris, 2009

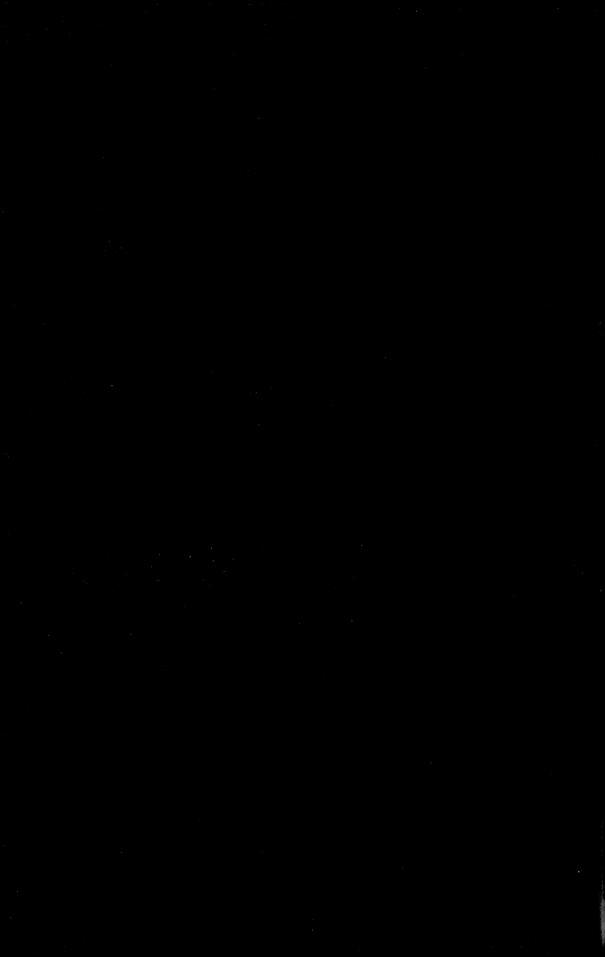

END OF THE THEATER, BEGINNING OF HUMAN MECHANICS.

—Jean Baudrillard, *Symbolic Exchange and Death*, 1993

CONTENTS

I DON'T LIKE DOING PICTURES AS MYSELF. I LIKE TO BE MADE INTO SOMEBODY DIFFERENT. IN A PICTURE, IT'S HARD TO BE YOURSELF. BUT WHEN YOU'RE PRETENDING TO BE SOMEONE ELSE, IT'S NICE. IT'S FUN. IT'S MORE INTERESTING.

—Kate Moss, *Interview*, March 1999

INTRODUCTION
SO KATE

DURING A RARE 2006 INTERVIEW, the editor-in-chief of American *Vogue*, Anna Wintour, boldly stated: "If you look at any great fashion photograph out of context, it will tell you just as much about what's going on in the world as a headline in the *New York Times*."[1] If Anna Wintour is right, Kate Moss's iconography, with photographs of her flooding the planet since 1990, constitutes a precious source of information about the world today. At the very least, this iconography is an irreplaceable testament to our times.

Icon, Muse, or Myth?

The first contact with Kate Moss is quantitative. It includes her astronomical personal wealth, her countless magazine covers, the numerous brands to which she has lent her face, and the many years she has spent at the top of the modeling world. Whatever the subject, Kate Moss beats records—of success, scandal, longevity, notoriety, money amassed, famous lovers, and alcohol consumption. She is the most-photographed, most-copied model and—along with Gisele Bündchen and Heidi Klum—one of the three best paid in the world. Whether looking into her personality, her business, or her talent, one always finds Moss "too" something: too cool, too skinny, too rich, too beautiful, too scandalous. Her legend is built on excess.

Kate Moss is a long string of logos, a succession of famous names. She has appeared not only on three hundred *Vogue* covers, as well as multiple covers for *Harper's Bazaar*, *Elle*, and *Vanity Fair*, but also in hundreds of editorial fashion stories in the most avant-garde British and American magazines such as *Another Man*, *The Face*, and *W*, all of which anticipate fashion trends and sometimes manufacture them. Moss has modeled for the best fashion photographers: Helmut Newton, Richard Avedon, Corinne Day, Patrick Demarchelier, Mario Sorrenti, Juergen Teller, and Mario Testino. She has followed stylists and designers such as Melanie Ward, John Galliano, and Alexander McQueen, and has represented the most prestigious couture houses: Yves Saint Laurent, Chanel, Calvin Klein, Longchamp, Burberry, Louis Vuitton, Stella McCartney, Gucci, Dolce & Gabbana, Versace, Dior, and Bulgari.

In the early twenty-first century, Moss has become a contemporary-art and pop-culture icon. Portraits of her have been exhibited in galleries and museums. Lucian Freud, perhaps the greatest British painter alive, painted one of them. Journalist Jonathan Jones expressed surprise in an April 2006 article in the British daily *The Guardian* that people would be bent on painting a portrait of such a "hollow" figure. Jones deplored "the death of British art," which has made her its muse. But this phenomenon is a paradox in appearance only. For while Moss is indeed a hollow figure whose legend needs ever-new characters to give it form and life—and this hollowing-out of the self has taken the shape of this mythically skinny girl unfairly associated with anorexia nervosa—Moss is no anomaly in our system. Rather, she is its ideal type. She is the integrated rebel. She takes full

responsibility for her excesses. She does not transgress codes as much as personify a new, contradictory code in which transgression is the social norm.

Manager and Cinderella

What might have been so fascinating about Moss that Marc Jacobs, a designer who was not even aware of her name in summer 1990, pinned one of her covers for *The Face* on his wall—the one in which Moss is topless, wearing a Native American headdress and a rather contracted grin on her lips? Was it the indeterminate aspect of a child's anatomy in which signs of femininity were detectable, or the sexual ambiguity of the androgynous morphological type that fashion and the movies had been cultivating since the postwar years? Was Kate Moss a reincarnation of Vladimir Nabokov's and Stanley Kubrick's Lolita, or of Twiggy, the lanky model who was discovered in a hair salon in 1966 and became famous for her thinness, weighing in at ninety pounds at age sixteen? The child of a carpenter and a supermarket cashier, Twiggy, like Moss, came from a London suburb. As Moss would later assert when asked about her origins, she came from a more-or-less comfortable middle-class milieu—adding, self-deprecatingly, "Middling middle-class."[2]

This is precisely what distinguishes Moss from another androgynous figure, Audrey Hepburn, who for her part was aristocratic, the daughter of a Dutch baroness and a British father, and received a strict education at a British boarding school. Reinventing herself in the fashion and film business in the postwar years after abandoning dreams of becoming a dancer, Hepburn would go on to embody the cheeky, dynamic face of the liberated modern woman.

In 2003, American artist Alex Katz attempted an explanation: "[Moss] is completely ordinary. That's what makes her extraordinary."[3] There's something about this girl, and "It's not just beauty," photographer Mario Testino opined in an article in French *Vogue* in late 2005. "She has personality, taste, humor. She has a universe you want to belong to, and when you're with her, in some way you feel like you are living more intensely. There are people like that. You get the feeling that their lives are more exciting than ours, a bit more fascinating, a bit more blessed by the gods."[4] According to Katherine Kendall, Moss's American biographer, these are contradictions that explain Moss's

Page 1: Kate Moss on the runway for Louis Vuitton's Fall/Winter 2012 presentation. Page 12: Various magazine advertisements and covers featuring Kate Moss, September 2006. Moss appeared in a record number of advertising campaigns that fall, one year after losing numerous major contracts as a result of tabloid photographs of her purportedly snorting a white powder in 2005. Opposite: Moss at a Calvin Klein presentation at Macy's Herald Square, New York City, 1994.

15

resonance in our time. She is at once "accessible and unapproachable, vulnerable and strong, real and fantastic, delicate and fierce, sexual and androgynous."[5]

Countless profiles of her in the press depict her as at once sturdy and fragile, ordinary and extraordinary, nomadic and rooted, a manufactured object and a myth from heaven, possessing an inimitable style and capable of representing a dizzying succession of logos: her chameleonlike beauty allows her to change her appearance without losing the ability to be recognized. Everything about her is "so Kate," a tautological definition that masks the very difficulty of defining her. All of Moss's biographies recount this game of oppositions over and over again: the abandoned child and the God-chosen one, the star and the girl next door, the kid from a London suburb and the global nomad, the manager of millions by age twenty and the Cinderella visited by a fairy godmother. She is "hype," she is "fun," she is "cool"—that's a given. She mixes genres, styles, and many other things as well. She is the Keith Richards of modeling, an icon of coolness, a serious contender to Diana, Princess of Wales's title of "the People's Princess." And above all, she can sell—dresses, jewels, magazines, and beauty products.

Opposite: Moss and Karl
Lagerfeld backstage at Lagerfeld's
ready-to-wear presentation,
Spring/Summer 1995.
Above: A Chanel advertisement
for Coco Mademoiselle featuring
Moss, September 2005.

Her influence, which has kept increasing over the years, is not linked to the prestige of the brands she represents. It is she who imparts her magnetism to them, not the other way around. She is neither the ambassador of a single style, as was the case with Coco Chanel, nor is she a sex symbol like Marilyn Monroe. "Rebel and incandescent, the British model gives rise to all kinds of passions," claimed French weekly *L'Express* in a December 2006 profile of Kate Moss penned by novelist Marie Desplechin.[6]

Moss makes superlatives dance. Everything suits her: the clothes she wears as well as the cultural signs she attracts. Operating as if by magic, she is a phenomenon of language as much as an icon of popular culture.

Writings of a Legend

It is a constant of the biographies of artists and stars: episodes claiming to be "real" or "truthful" most often draw from the same stock of recurring scenes and images, the function of which is to explain the unexplainable, the apparition of an exceptional figure among humans.

Moss and Johnny Depp at Mickey
Rourke's thirty-eighth birthday party,
New York City, September 1994.

In the 1930s, two art historians, Ernst Kris and Otto
Kurz, conducted a systematic study of artist biographies
from antiquity to the Italian Renaissance.[7] They made a
surprising discovery: known episodes in the lives of these
artists belonged to a stock of images and representations
that were identical to those developed in antiquity. Among
them was the fated figure, with its telling signs, its omens,
a vocation born, a precocious genius discovered by another
artist, the typical "mere child's play." The same goes for
the lives of our stars, including actors and models. The

construction of the Kate Moss myth by her biographers draws on the same stock of recurring images.

From her childhood in a southern suburb of London to her discovery at age fourteen at New York's John F. Kennedy Airport by Sarah Doukas, founder and owner of Storm Model Management and her first agent; from photographer Corinne Day's methodical construction of the waif figure (the abandoned child) for magazines such as *The Face* and *Harper's Bazaar* to her entering the world of supermodels, where she would be enthroned as a luxury-brand figurehead, the Moss legend tells a true success story: that of a middle-class teenager who would become one of the best-paid models in the world with no apparent effort. Her journey is spiced up by tumultuous episodes (famous lovers, including actor Johnny Depp, Babyshambles and Libertines singer Pete Doherty, and guitarist Jamie Hince of the Kills), themselves interrupted by stays in rehab, controversies about her reputed addictions, and front-page tabloid scandals. Hers is a legend that reveals less about her personality than it does about how a collective myth is written.

"Many extraordinary stories have ordinary beginnings," writes Angela Buttolph, the author of *Kate Moss Style: Inside the World's Most Famous Wardrobe*.[8] "And life doesn't get more ordinary than British suburbia. Croydon, in South London, is a bleak concrete tangle of tower blocks, gray office complexes, ugly shopping centers, and endless roundabouts. Not exactly the natural environment in which to nurture a world-class style icon. But it was here that Katherine Ann Moss was born on 16 January 1974."

Thus it is difficult to tackle the Kate Moss phenomenon without paraphrasing a legend that is already written. Moss's biographies often fall into a legend-rewriting trap, with scenes repeated ad infinitum, the same fateful characters, the same legendary destiny. It is not Kate Moss's life biographers are writing about but rather an already written legend that is retold in the same manner, in a loop that constitutes what cultural sociologists call "the enchanted circle of legitimacy." Everything happens to her as if in a fairy tale, without her intending any of it, simply by her making herself available, open, and adaptable, and welcoming with utter simplicity her fabulous destiny as a model. "The lives that unfold without anyone feeling their authors shed blood and tears that unfold almost in spite of their authors—these lives are sublime," opines Moss's French biographer, Françoise-Marie Santucci of the French daily *Libération*.[9]

A Vamp, Not a Vampire

There is the visible Kate, a flood of deliberately created or stolen images traveling the Internet in a big, unruly mess somewhere between pornography and fashion, celebrity rags and contemporary art. And then there's the legible Kate, a stock of biographical anecdotes told over and over again in the tabloids to the point of surfeit, in women's magazines, and in biographies. Here's Kate's body, photographed from every angle imaginable, and the body of her written lives, a kaleidoscope of anecdotes and scandals located halfway between the society pages and fashion sociology.

From her trashing of luxury hotel suites with Johnny Depp to the stolen images of her doing drugs with Pete Doherty (earning her the nickname "Cocaine Kate"), from evenings spent drinking and hanging out with model girlfriends in London, Milan, and Paris during the cities' fashion weeks to the orgiastic parties that tabloids like to report on or fantasize about—such as her thirtieth birthday, during which she was reportedly costumed as a pagan princess and very high—Kate Moss is a written-about woman, a woman with stories and new developments, a living chronicle, a series of interlocking anecdotes, lovers, characters, and scripts. The multiple scenes of transgression that are part of her so-called rock-and-roll look partake of a legend built on the profanation of an image of innocence and purity. With her, the eternal feminine becomes secular; drifting from the sacred to the profane, and from the profane to profanation.

"I married a vamp, not a vampire," playwright Arthur Miller once allegedly quipped, mocking Marilyn Monroe and her self-destructive tendencies. This remark is said to have made Marilyn laugh, probably because she knew that if a vampire were in fact hovering over the couple, she would be its first victim. For Miller, the Marilyn phenomenon was the point where personal pathology met the insatiable appetite of a capitalist culture of consumption. He characterized this encounter as a mystery, but also as an obscenity. This definition might be extended to Kate Moss. But while Arthur Miller, who had been Marilyn's husband—and may have had the ambition of being her therapist—was somewhat entitled to speak about her pathology, in following the same path we may be at risk of yielding to what the late French sociologist, anthropologist, and philosopher Pierre Bourdieu used to call "the biographical illusion."[10]

Warhol vs. Banksy, screenprint on paper, Banksy, 2005. This limited edition print of Moss was inspired by Andy Warhol's screenprints of Marilyn Monroe. Moss's copy of the print was stolen from her London home in 2010.

For biography is of no help in understanding a person who has become a social phenomenon, given that she herself is a social construction. Furthermore, in the tabloids, that person easily becomes a pure and simple list of ills: in Kate Moss's case, alleged addiction and imaginary anorexia.

Looking for Kate Moss behind the masks woven by legend would be in vain. "So much gossip had circulated about me," said Moss as early as 1994. "What they wrote was so stupid that I never bothered responding. And the more visible they make me, the more invisible I become."[11] Kate Moss is a composite object, a mixture put together by fashion and magazines; a kind of plastic social "braid" that weaves together the "values" of our time like so many plastic threads: youth, speed, transgression; the ability to play a role and attract attention; a mimetic power that would turn this frail teenager into a formidable agent for prescription. "I'm just a model," she ceaselessly repeats to avoid being petrified by her legend. But being a model in the 1990s is no small thing. As Bret Easton Ellis wrote in the novel *Glamorama*, a model helps "define the decade, baby."[12]

1

A BLUE FLOWER IN THE LAND OF TECHNOLOGY

————————————————————————
————————————————————————
————————————————————————
————————————————————————
————————————————————————

HERE SHE IS RUNNING, SWIMMING cap on her head, in dark blue shorts with white stripes on the side. There she is walking, clumsily hiding her nakedness, one arm hiding her breasts, the other pressing a large straw hat over her pubis, like a swimmer coming out of the water and hurrying to get dry. The next photograph is practically identical; only the angle is different. In another image, she is sitting on the floor, wearing a raffia skirt that reveals her naked legs; she is still laughing, but differently this time, as if she had just been forced to—is this modesty or a fit of hysterical laughter from a young girl on vacation? Here she is leaning against a wall, pensive, with her arms crossed, a vintage vest against her skin; she is smoking the way adolescents do, with seriousness and application, as if smoking were an activity in itself. In another picture, she is moving toward the camera, a large necklace covering her bare breasts, eyes squinting against too much light. The following image frames her freckled face more tightly, but she is no longer laughing: she is staring at the lens sternly, her gaze suddenly heavy with worry, or perhaps she is just eager to not disappoint the girlfriend photographing her.

Finally there is the most famous of these photographs, the one that made it to the June 1990 cover of *The Face*: wearing a Native American headdress, her nose wrinkled, Moss is laughing, completely amazed to be here, bare-breasted on a wind-beaten beach, when she really should be in school.

An Imperfect Beauty

If one were not able recognize Kate Moss's pointy canines, beauty spots, and tabloid-worthy leanness, these black-and-white photographs—soon to be famous the world over—might be featured in any album full of ageless sepia-toned pictures framed by wavy borders and held in place by transparent corners. In this album one might find the same freshness, the same innocence, and above all, the same joy that each generation of children feels in front of the camera upon first discovering the miracle of photography.

The precise date of these photographs is unknown. Some people claim they were made one freezing afternoon in September 1989, others claim it was in spring 1990—it was before June, in any case, as they were published in the pages of *The Face*'s special summer issue. By contrast, the location is very well known: Camber Sands in East Sussex, south of London, is an ideal beach for nautical sports requiring space and wind. In summer, one might see windsurfers gliding on the water or skateboards and buggies, their sails taut with wind, racing through the dunes. The place is also a favorite among film production companies, which find the dunes an ideal landscape for desert scenes and war movies like *The Longest Day*, filmed here in the early 1960s. Commercials, video clips, fashion photographs, and big-budget movies with hundreds of extras are made here as well.

Yet on this day the beach is empty. There are no blinding movie lights or silver reflecting panels. No tungsten lamps or white umbrellas. The only perceptible noises are the shutter's claps and shots from a nearby military base shooting range. There's no point looking for an army of assistants and lighting designers, or for heavy-production four-wheel drives stuck in the sand. On this beach beaten by a freezing wind are a girl wearing a T-shirt and two girlfriends who never take their eyes off her.

Kate Moss is here with photographer Corinne Day and stylist Melanie Ward (now a designer in her own right), who made a habit of combing the Camden and Portobello flea markets for second-hand and vintage clothes and accessories. There was no way the great couture houses would lend clothes, as the three young warriors are complete unknowns in the fashion business. And in any case, what ex-model Corinne Day is looking for stands in stark opposition to 1980s glamour. From the fashion milieu she used to frequent, Day remembers a world where

Page 22: Martine Sitbon ready-to-wear presentation, Fall/Winter circa 1994. Opposite, top and bottom: Moss backstage at a Paris fashion presentation, 1991.

"artifice was the only thing people swore by," Françoise-Marie Santucci reports. "It was all about shoulder pads, blush, and makeup. But I didn't want to show the girls in a glamorous light. I wanted to instill a bit of reality into a world of fantasy."[13] In Milan, where Day had collaborated with the Italian branch of the Elite modeling agency, she had already found that "the girls were much prettier when hanging out at home in pajamas, smoking pot, and drinking a glass of wine."[14]

The model as a symbol of perfection reached its heyday in the 1980s, but became by the close of the decade an almost banal and superficial ideal. By wanting so much to conform to a "perfect" beauty defined by weight and measurement norms, a feminine ideal had been created that was inaccessible, but without surprises. "For the last three years, it had been the same girls on the covers of magazines," Marilyn Gauthier, whose Marilyn Agency represents Moss in France, later confessed to the weekly, Le Nouvel Observateur, "Enough! We had to get out of that rut. A beautiful chest is no longer fashionable. Cindy Crawford? Nothing is more 'out' than that look. Fortunately for her, Cindy is making exercise videos in the United States; she's reinvented herself."[15] "You couldn't go any further than 'supermodels,'" added New York designer Anna Sui. "You couldn't get any taller, blonder, or breastier."[16]

With the dawn of the 1990s came time for a type of beauty that was more real, free of foundation, blush, and hairspray. For an entire generation of young photographers, only imperfection seemed new and exciting. "Having dark circles under her eyes doesn't make a woman ugly," said Day. "It's just a different kind of beauty."[17]

Kate Investigated

The meeting between the budding fifteen-year-old model and the then-budding photographer Corinne Day, her elder by only ten years, went beyond a simple professional collaboration. As the young photographer would later explain, it was a mirror relationship: "I think there was a bit of narcissism there because she was 5'7" and skinny like me. I'd been tortured at school for my shape, and had a hard time for it as a model. I thought she'd have some of the problems I've had, and wanted to help."[18]

After spending a decade traveling to Japan, Thailand, Italy, and the United States, by the end of the 1980s, Corinne

Anne Klein ready-to-wear,
Fall/Winter 1994–95.

Day settled in London. She tried to find her bearings and
revisited her difficult childhood: she was raised by her
grandmother in the suburbs, her father gone, her mother
a prostitute. It was a perfect biography for what would
become a look in fashion of which Kate Moss would be
the prototype: the waif. Except that for her part, Moss had
a rather easy childhood, a kind of hippie education with a
stay-at-home mother who listened to the Rolling Stones and
liked flower-print skirts and a travel-agent father who spent
his time looking for discount travel packages for his kids'
vacations, preferably in tropical climes.

In Kate Moss, Corinne Day had found much more than a model: she had found a double. For Moss, Day would be both a mirror and a gentle guide taking her along on a diving expedition into her childhood's buried landscapes. Day took Moss to Ickenham, the suburb where she grew up. She photographed Moss in the small backyard of her grandmother's detached house, in the park where she played as a child. She took her to the flea market where both of them tried on all kinds of costumes, as young girls do. They also traveled together, retracing the steps Corinne had taken when she was fleeing her past. From Borneo, Day brought back images of Kate coming out of the water with her hair wet, flippers on, surrounded by local children. Day did not ask Moss to pose. She did not direct her but rather accompanied her as closely as she could, on the lookout for her expressions, seeking to capture the bizarre yet radiant image of a teenager who looked like her sister and whom she described as being insolent and incredibly self-assured, yet still a child who might break into heavy sobs over the smallest thing.

In the pictures published in *The Face*, Kate Moss appeared without mask or makeup and with a childlike naïveté that came through in the slightly forced laughter that wrinkled her nose. The images were likely the result of Moss's lack of experience, but were also Day's intention. "I wanted to just photograph her as herself, to try and get it as documentary as possible. And get her character and her presence in the picture. Because fashion [photography] really wasn't about that in the 80s, it was all about the photographer."[19] In fact, these no-frills shots, in black and white, belonged with the documentary style of photography more than they did in fashion photography, with their natural light, apparent spontaneity of gesture and gaze, and lack of retouching of lines and shadows during their development and printing. Corinne Day was investigating Kate as well as herself and an entire generation. She was questioning the limits of childhood and adulthood, the boundaries of the feminine genre. "Clothes and makeup are not the subject with Kate. The subject is her," Day would say later on. "I have always done her portrait in a style that is close to documentary. This realism suits her better than any other model."[20]

The charm of these photographs depends entirely on the unstable balance between mastery and spontaneity, work and play. As in a photo-story, one reads through a sequence of frozen images that seem to be hopscotching in time, jumping lightly from one pose to the next, creating as many questions as answers in attempting to define an enigma of presence and beauty. Reality is summoned here, but—as we have known since the beginnings of photography—the nakedness of the immediate can be revealed only by the greatest of artifice. This is how the Kate Moss phenomenon was to bloom at the beginning of the 1990s, like a "Blue Flower in the land of technology," in Walter Benjamin's striking definition.[21] The shy teenager would become the face of a generation. Her work with Corinne Day, Moss would later say, "captured what was going on in England at the time."[22]

The Third Summer of Love

The Face was a magazine dedicated to exploring musical and aesthetic trends, and these first published photographs of Moss are now famous for launching a new era in fashion photography and identifying the spirit of a new generation. As a matter of fact, their publication signaled the breaking out of Generation X, as characterized by writer Douglas Coupland in his novel *Generation X: Tales for an Accelerated Culture.*[23]

For once, the idea of a generation was not a mere media construction. You could see it embodied in the streets, dancing at rave parties under the spell of a new synthetic drug, Ecstasy, which was said to induce empathy and anorexia. Suckled on the milk of video clips broadcast the world over by MTV—which, created at the beginning of the 1980s, contributed to the formatting of musical tastes and clothing styles—Generation Xers stormed through Western capitals like members of a carnival that ruffled aesthetic habits, flipped the categories "beautiful" and "ugly," blurred the lines between genres, imposed a form of corrosive irony that attacked the codes of glamour, and preached hybridization and nostalgia as remedies for shaken identities. Titled "The Third Summer of Love" in homage to the hippie movement of summer 1967, *The Face*'s special summer issue positioned itself as a response to the flower-power revolution. Rave parties had replaced rock festivals; Ecstasy, pot; electronic music, pop music; and vintage clothes, printed calico skirts and flowered shirts. Using a few simple words, Kate Moss expressed the ethos of the time: "Everybody was saying, 'Let's get off our tits and have a laugh. Be more real and not have to grow up so quickly. And have fun.'"[24]

The fall of the Berlin Wall in 1989 had precipitated the end of the twentieth century before the twenty-first had even begun—for this to happen, one would have to wait until September 11, 2001. Meanwhile, pundits had officially declared "the end of history," a famous phrase political economist Francis Fukuyama had initially coined as a title for an article in the summer 1989 issue of the *National Interest* magazine. This period was a sort of intermission or halftime between two centuries, and it would last a full decade. Anyone who came of age between these two dates would have to wait. This was the end of totalitarianism, nuclear deterrence, and a division of the world established at Yalta; it was a time when both the avant-garde and the political declined.

Stuck in suspended time, the generation that reached adulthood in the 1990s found itself in a zero-gravity narrative. The decade was ten years of regression—"of thawing," as Jean Baudrillard would later put it.[25] The death of "grand narratives," in the words of French philosopher Jean-François Lyotard,[26] whose complex thinking was reduced to postmodern catechism, became the key phrase, and the "quest for meaning" a quasi-religious duty, with applications into the realm of management.

Acting as so many tributaries, the multiplication of small narratives of adaptation in all fields of social life merged into the storytelling mainstream, whose flow kept increasing through the 1990s until it flooded corporate management, marketing, political and institutional communications, therapy, law, and professional and military training.[27] Far from acting as a remedy, these instrumental uses of narratives would only underline the major symptom of the century's end: the absence or impossibility of a narrative.

Anekdiegesis: Experience without Narrative

As early as the 1930s, in a famous essay titled "The Storyteller," Walter Benjamin had examined the crisis of narration between the two world wars, identified as a decline in the ability to tell stories, which the Greeks had previously characterized as *anekdiegesis*.[28] According to Benjamin, peoples' and individuals' narrative competence would regress to the point of disappearance when their experience ceased to be communicable. "One reason for this phenomenon is obvious," Benjamin explained. "Experience has fallen in value. And it looks as if it is continuing to fall into bottomlessness…. For never has

Opposite: Versace Haute Couture, Spring/Summer 1996. **Pages 34–35, from left to right:** Callaghan ready-to-wear, Spring/Summer 1993; Istante ready-to-wear, Spring/Summer 1994; Chanel ready-to-wear, Fall/Winter 1997–98; Vivienne Westwood ready-to-wear, Spring/Summer 1995.

experience been contradicted more thoroughly than strategic experience by tactical warfare, economic experience by inflation, bodily experience by mechanical warfare, moral experience by those in power."[29]

That phenomenon occurred again in the 1980s and 1990s. The strategic experience of dissuasion was thoroughly contradicted by the end of the Cold War. The economic experience of globalization was beginning to relocate millions of jobs, deepening inequalities, and favoring financial deregulation. The experience of sexual liberation was contradicted by the appearance of AIDS, which raised anew the specter of a pandemic. The experience of progress was contradicted by severe ecological disturbances as well as the first large nuclear catastrophe in 1986 in Chernobyl, which prompted Europe to first unite under the same nuclear cloud before it could reunite with the fall of the Berlin Wall. It was not solely levels of experience that were contradicted by facts, as Benjamin observed in his time, but the possibility of a real experience of the body, which was being put into question by genetic mutations, cloning, neuroscience, and biotechnology. As for men and women's experiences of time and space, unchanged until then, they were now reduced to ridicule by the globalization of the media, new information and communication technologies, and the explosion of the Internet.

The introduction by television of "instantaneous" modes of narration, which cable and news channels made into a massive global means of conveying experience, resulted in a decisive worsening of narration. Benjamin had observed this phenomenon in the 1930s, when it was the result of the creation of the modern press.

A Situation of Narrative Impasse

In *Generation X*, a novel that would mirror a generation maturing in a situation of narrative impasse, Douglas Coupland established a clinical portrait of the neo-anekdiegesis of the 1990s. His prognosis was in sharp contrast to the usual clichés about lost generations, all of which are usually full of statistics about downward mobility, anxiety about joblessness, consumerism, brand-consciousness, and drug addiction. Very early on in the novel, a character expresses the general symptom Coupland had so clearly identified: "It's not healthy to live life as a succession of isolated little cool moments.... We know that this is why the three of us left our lives behind us and came to the desert—to tell stories and to make our own lives worthwhile tales in the process."[30]

A few years earlier, the French philosopher Paul Ricoeur had published *Time and Narrative*,[31] a philosophical summation in three volumes that used the notions of intrigue and temporality to conceptualize the idea of a narrative construction of personal identity. Ricoeur's book was not lacking for insight and aptness. Yet in the final analysis, it seemed a bit tardy and obvious. "Most of us have only two or three genuinely interesting moments in our lives," Coupland wrote. "The rest is just filler, and ... at the end of our lives, most of us will be lucky if any of those moments connect together to form a story that anyone would find remotely interesting."[32]

How might this hunger for stories, this addiction to stories, be sated, other than by stories of addiction? Coupland viewed Alcoholics Anonymous meetings as the ultimate survival of campfire evenings, the last flicker of narration in a mute and desperate society. "AA members want to hear the horror stories of how far you've sunk in life, and no low is low enough. Tales of spouse abuse, embezzlement, and public incontinence are both appreciated and expected. I know this as a fact because I've been to these meetings (lurid details of my own life will follow at a later date), and I've seen the process of one-downmanship in action—and been angry at not having sordid enough tales of debauchery of my own to share.... Thus inspired by my meetings of the Alcoholics Anonymous organization, I instigated a policy of storytelling in my own life, a policy of 'bedtime stories,' which [we] share among ourselves."[33]

Sixteen years later, writer Don DeLillo would give an account of this situation of narrative impasse in his 2007 novel *Falling Man*. The device he chose to observe the process of self-degradation through narrative was not AA meetings but a group of men and women with Alzheimer's disease. Lianne, the wife of a World Trade Center attack survivor, takes part in storyline sessions with six or seven men and women in the early stages of the disease. With great detail, DeLillo described the disease's relentless progression as if it were a metaphor for our times: "They wrote for roughly twenty minutes and then each, in turn, read aloud what he or she had written.

Sometimes it scared her, the first signs of a halting response, the losses and failings, the grim prefigurings that issued now and then from a mind beginning to slide away from the adhesive friction that makes an individual possible. It was in the language, the inverted letters, the lost word at the end of a struggling sentence. It was in the handwriting that might melt into runoff."[34]

From AA meetings to storyline sessions for Alzheimer's patients, these therapeutic uses of narration constituted the alarming symptom of a fabulating function gone awry, one that no longer bore witness to the narrative construction of identity so dear to Paul Ricoeur, but rather to the individual's narrative degradation, all the way to the affected brain sliding "away from the adhesive friction that makes an individual possible."

In a survival reflex, Coupland's Generation Xers invented Texlahoma, an imaginary country where they could set their stories, a place that could be easily confused with Facebook and Second Life's virtual universes peopled by tribes of friends or costumed avatars. In a world detached from the real, the only rules were that interrupting and criticizing were forbidden: "This noncritical atmosphere works for us.... A clause like this was the only way we could feel secure with each other."[35] This involuntary confession revealed the link between the return of the narrative and the abandonment of all critical thinking. "It's a sad Everyplace, where citizens are always getting fired from their jobs at 7-Eleven and where the kids do drugs and practice the latest dance crazes at the local lake, where they also fantasize about being adults and pulling welfare-check scams.... Life is boring there, but there are some thrills to be had: all adults keep large quantities of cheaply sewn sex garments in their chests of drawers."[36]

The Bible of Cool

At that time, Corinne Day was not the only person to advocate a realistic anti-glamour direction for fashion. Her work belonged to what would be called the "London School," which included photographers such as David Sims, Juergen Teller, and Nigel Shafran. All of them would become known through a new kind of press, represented by such magazines as *The Face*, *i-D*, *Blitzed*, and *Dazed & Confused*. The photographers shared not just an intentional documentary style but also a rejection of the sophisticated shooting techniques that had made the construction of ideal images of beauty possible. Their rise would hasten the demise of the "natural healthy" look, embodied by 1980s supermodels Cindy Crawford and Claudia Schiffer, in favor of a *moda povera*, waif, or grunge look, in which styles and cultures were mixed and blasé attitudes made daily life heroic.

Soon nicknamed the "Bible of Cool," *The Face*—whose figurehead Kate Moss would become—was launched in 1980 by former music critic Nick Logan. Initially, *The Face* was a rock magazine, but it had already defined itself as "the world's best-dressed magazine." Between 1981 and 1995, its circulation hovered between 56,000 and 75,000, then decreased steadily toward the turn of the new century. A victim of its own success, the magazine was competing with too many imitators and eventually closed in May 2004.

The Face was a contemporary of the 1989–2001 historical parenthesis we have characterized as a narrative impasse, with all the term implies about formalist complacency, escape into kitsch, and the aestheticization of psychological and cultural misery. In some respect, *The Face* was the official publication of the Republic of Texlahoma, where Generation Xers—with their dreams that had not come true, their rejection of the world, and their nostalgia for purity—had sought refuge. Never had a generation been so anxious to define itself, to narrate itself even before it had lived, and worse, with the acute awareness of the impossibility of living real experiences. This generation was crushed by the awareness both of its narrative identity and of the impossibility of realizing it, condemned as it was to produce substitute narratives to replace real experience.

The contents of these new magazines were not limited to the worlds of fashion and music: creating the "mood" of a time and "constructing an attitude" that would be characterized as grunge (dirty, messy) were also on the menu. As a musical style, grunge emerged on the Seattle scene and soon applied to the entire youth culture with the release of Nirvana's 1991 album *Nevermind*—just as "cool" had done in the 1980s. Grunge came to characterize an entire series of cultural practices: the emergence of new designers like Alexander McQueen and John Galliano; trendy brands; new cultural scenes; the Camden and Portobello flea markets; rave parties held on the periphery of cities; new drugs like Ecstasy; bands like the Stone Roses and the Happy Mondays; films like *Trainspotting*; David Foster Wallace's novel *Infinite Jest* and Coupland's *Generation X*.

Opposite, top: Romeo Gigli ready-to-wear, Spring/Summer 1995.
Opposite, bottom: Calvin Klein ready-to-wear, Spring/Summer 1996.

A most useful catch-all category, grunge described a generation's modes of consumption, a musical style, a syntax, and a way of dressing that a magazine like *The Face* attempted to decipher: "The moment seemed ideal to us," wrote journalist Sheryl Garratt, a former *Face* editor, in the December 2005–January 2006 issue of French *Vogue*. "A new generation of designers and photographers was beginning to show their work.... They preferred models who looked 'real,' and whose imperfection they underlined rather than retouched."[37]

Every aspect of popular culture was interesting to *The Face*. In a single issue, one could find a feature about New York's rap culture, photographs of the Hassidic Jewish community and its traditional clothing, and a report about Bollywood's kitsch extravagance—all in a layout inspired by Russian constructivism. British professor Paul Jobling inventoried the themes found in the magazine between 1985 and 1996: they were gender, race, and nationality; sexuality, androgyny, aliens, the waif look, anti-fashion trends, and fetishism. Also to be found were film reviews as well as articles about surrealism, history, nostalgia, and the turn of the third millennium.

This postmodern eclecticism attracted Baudrillardian criticism from the left-leaning photography journal *Ten.8*, which found that *The Face* was blurring the lines between politics, parody, and pastiche, and that it was prioritizing style over substance. According to the *Ten.8* critic, *The Face* was ignoring the social reality it claimed it was documenting, instead only proposing a world of floating signs in which "history is played and played over again like a ludic succession of styles, genres, and significant practices that can be combined and recombined at will. No learning. No class. No history. Just an endless procession of simulacra."[38]

Decade Blending

▬▬▬

For Texlahoma's inhabitants, as for the citizens of Second Life, making one's life into a story meant jerry-rigging composite identities from accessories and signs borrowed from the fashions of previous decades. This was what Coupland called "decade blending," which he defined as follows: "the indiscriminate combination of two or more items from various decades to create a

personal mood: Sheila = Mary Quant earrings (1960s) +
cork wedge platform shoes (1970s) + black leather jacket
(1950s and 1980s)."

Flea markets—these gigantic cemeteries of past
fashions haunted by costumed ghosts—would become
a favorite hunting ground for such "decade blending." For
young stylists like Melanie Ward, being able to rummage
through clothes from different styles and periods at a
single stall was a constant source of inspiration and an
incentive to imagine new combinations. Within a single
day, one might find a multicolored suede waistcoat with
fringes from the 1970s, a Harris tweed riding suit, or a
black gabardine one from the 1940s, and compose eclectic
mélanges by mixing threadbare 1930s dresses with
sneakers, and cashmere sweaters with elbow holes with
overly long bias-cut pants.

Styles were mixed, and so were sizes and propor-
tions: short shorts were paired with long coats, extra-long
covered sleeves with sleeveless T-shirts, low-waisted
jeans with floor-sweeping flares. And because clothes
were cheap, no one hesitated to transform them with a
few clips of the scissors or to associate them in a completely anachronistic manner. It was a new attitude, free
of complexes, taboos, and veneration. According to
Melanie Ward, "there were no boundaries between day
or night, or expensive and cheap. In a way we completely
redefined a new sophistication."[39] This sophistication was
paradoxical, for it consisted of a valorization of the "banal"
and a turn away from sculptural figureheads and toward
new models with a novel, insolent, and imperfect beauty
that came from the street.

The influence of *The Face* and *i-D*, its competitor,
was felt most of all in editorial fashion pages ("the
straight up") that were wholly independent from haute
couture ads. Instead of using professional models
in studio settings, these fashion stories, spread over
ten or so pages, showed anti-models photographed in
natural environments—streets, hangars, and beaches.
The images credited the brands their subjects wore
and the shops the clothes came from. Between 1980
and 1986, Nick Logan called upon about fifty young
photographers, most of whom had never been published
in major magazines such as *Vogue* and *Harper's Bazaar*,
to contribute to the magazine. Some became famous:
Juergen Teller, Nick Knight, David Sims, Paolo Roversi,
and Corinne Day among them.

Dirty Realism

"It wasn't 1980s glamour," Moss would say. "It was about the street." Out with luxuriant settings for otherworldly goddesses, in with ordinary men and women photographed on the streets. This new style reinforced the idea that the object of fashion was lifestyle, and that it now consisted in styling daily life. Iwona Blazwick, the director of London's Whitechapel Gallery—renowned for featuring artists such as Pablo Picasso, Frida Kahlo, Jackson Pollock, Mark Rothko, and Nan Goldin throughout the twentieth century—described the turn toward realism that was being embraced by the new generation of magazines and photographers: "Constructed tableaux are rejected for a truth located in the artless, the unstaged, semi-conscious, the sexually indeterminate and the pubescent—the slippages between socially prescribed roles."[40]

After spending decades pursuing perfection, these new looks celebrated the unfinished, the imperfect, the neglected. Hairstyles turned away from the rigid codes of perms and blow-outs, and strove to simulate the natural, even the "disheveled"—these "natural" effects being achieved, of course, with hairspray and gel. These new codes became so much a part of the mores that big cosmetic brands now offered highly rigid sprays and gels for men who were keen on "unstyled" hairstyles for day and night.

Makeup reinforced dark shadows under eyes. Far from making faces look more beautiful or younger, it aimed to give an impression of abandonment, fatigue, or distress. The new canons of beauty no longer depended on strict norms for measurement, but rather on the body's trials, its marks and stigmas, its dark shadows and its lines. All this would be called "dirty realism," a busted-up form of beauty, fragile and threatened, in which the body was the hero, not the clothes; the body no longer transfigured by clothes but rather disfigured by trials, a victim to all manners of alterations and degradation; a suffering body that was being given a voice.

Eliding the garment in favor of the body took myriad forms—among them, the blurring that resulted from mixing styles. But garments could also be degraded and demystified when they were revealed as artifacts by showing seams and linings, by wearing them inside out, and by showing undergarments through the transparency of the garment that usually hid them. The garment was cut anew by visible scissor cuts; it was torn voluntarily. Consequently, the body itself became the object of fashion, not the garment, which disappeared to the point of becoming a simple accessory.

When the real disappears, nostalgia makes perfect sense, as Jean Baudrillard noted. And nostalgia then takes any shape possible. Fashion becomes a memorial, an archeology, a tomb of appearances. It summons signs of the past; it multiplies magical behaviors to resuscitate it. Fashion acts as if it were turning toward the real, but it is just dealing with defunct signs. Designer Alexander McQueen made "the body into a memento mori," noted Rebecca Arnold.[41] Confronted with an incredulous generation no longer fooled by the illusionism it represented, fashion would soon resort to exhibiting the body's wounds in order to be recognized, just like Ulysses did in Ithaca.

Fabled Bodies, Embodied Narratives

A photograph by Juergen Teller illustrates this phenomenon. The photograph was published on the cover of a *Süddeutsche Zeitung* supplement devoted to the themes of fashion and morals. In it, renowned model Kristen McMenamy stands naked, cigarette between her lips, a heart drawn in lipstick between her breasts, the word "Versace" written inside it. In this photograph, the brand is no longer attached to the garment, but to the body; a naked body that still bears the traces of a garment—jeans that were too tight around the waist, a zipper that crossed the groin—and that also shows signs of age or fatigue: a weary gaze, dark shadows under the eyes.

The half-burned cigarette between the lips, the hands on the hips, and the gaze staring down a possible voyeur leave no doubt: this portrait is not about eroticism and victimization. Juergen Teller chose to run counter to the watered-down images of the female body published in magazines, which he found odious: "They say Kristen McMenamy is a supermodel, and that's how they show her. I just wanted to say, listen, this is her."[42]

Kristen McMenamy the model was no less "artificial" when posing for Teller with the Versace label on her naked skin than when she walked the runway dressed in a haute couture dress. She was just as much "dressed" in signs, because she was modeling a representation of the female body located beyond maternal or sexual meanings. The strength of Teller's photograph lay in the effect of simulated reality, a challenge to which the real was defying fashion. A block of reality was radiating onto the label. The aura was being transferred from model to label. The "written body" could no longer be distinguished from the "image body," just like the "written garment" could no longer be distinguished from the "image garment" in Roland Barthes's *The Fashion System*. Both had fused in the figure of the "marked body," which bore the stigmas of its worldly peregrinations. In fact, tattoos were gradually invading parts of the body that had been abandoned by garments: multicolored frescoes would conquer the naked body, reaching shoulders made bare by décolletages, "dressing up" abdomens and backs bared by low-waisted jeans.

The "written body" certainly reached its zenith in Benetton's 1993 campaign, which covered the walls of large cities with posters showing naked AIDS patients whose skin bore the virus's acronym, HIV. Did Benetton want to express its anger at the stigmatization—the marking—from which AIDS patients suffered? Did it want to draw people's attention to a shameful disease? In any case, with this marking of the body, Benetton restored, perhaps involuntarily, the original meaning of "branding": the marking and identification techniques used for cattle. Critics saw the campaign as a profanation of the sick body. But focusing on the moral aspect of the question amounted to avoiding what was then fashion's formidable problem: decreased credibility in a society where everything could be "modeled." The garment was no longer enchanted. It had lost its showy splendor. Only the body could make signs dance.

Nostalgia is the uppermost feeling of a generation deprived of a future and forced to summon outmoded signs in a never-ending merry-go-round. It is then time to go back to origin stories, to a heightened quest for lived experience, to consciousness turned into narrative. For *The Face*'s young photographers, there existed no contradiction between "decade blending" à la Generation X and the quest for what was "natural," "true," and "experienced." The photographers were recording the death of real experience while cultivating its defunct signs. Similarly, there was no contradiction between the escape of Generation X's protagonists and the kind of "realism" advocated by Corinne Day: her quest for the real did not mean an all-out rejection of "artificial" signs in favor of raw reality; fiction and nonfiction belonged in the same universe of simulacrum. Everything was an act: the aesthetics of imperfection and recycling, the cult of vintage clothes, and the new attitudes (the waif and heroin chic) that Kate Moss was about to model pointed instead to a profusion of new signs, a production of dreamed or simulated images. "The real is dead," a precursory Jean Baudrillard announced in 1976, when his *Symbolic Exchange and Death* was first published. "Long live the realistic sign!"[43]

In photography as in film, immediate reality can be captured only through the greatest artifice. Not only because, as Walter Benjamin wrote, "In the film studio, the apparatus has penetrated so deeply into reality that a pure view of that reality, free of the foreign body of equipment, is the result of a special procedure, namely the shooting by the specially adjusted photographic device and the assembly of that shot with others of the same kind,"[44] but also because no reality exists that is not peopled by signs. Neither is there any nakedness that does not bear signs.

Corinne Day's neorealism wasn't an exception. The Native American headdress Kate Moss wore as her only garment was not there by chance: it was a nod to the world of stable identities, to Amerindian cultures close to nature. In fact, Kate Moss's iconography would continue to borrow from this "native" cultural lexicon synonymous with the natural, the innocent, and the authentic—all cardinal (and inverted) values in the kingdom of kitsch and artifice. The Native American is omnipresent in Moss's sign system, from felt moccasins to fringed suede vests, and from the prints used in her Topshop collections to the teepees she has erected in her garden. But this ethnic reference was not a sign pointing toward becoming a Native American identity. It bade good-bye to a lost world. It was a shroud or a scalp. And the young virgin wearing it was a ghost, or an apparition, that came back after casting off its worldly threads. For Corinne Day and the London School photographers, fashion was a tomb, the tomb of appearances.

Against a background of war and financial crisis, the ceremony of fashion no longer referred to an established order with rites, hierarchies, and distinctions; rather, it endeavored to express the precarious, fragile, and disintegrated nature of any identity.

Opposite, top: Chanel ready-to-wear, Spring/Summer 1997.
Opposite, bottom: Givenchy ready-to-wear, Spring/Summer 1997.

2
PURSUED BY WOLVES

IMAGINE KATE MOSS LOST AMONG the model's bucket brigade. Seamstresses, pins between their lips, were adjusting her pale blue striped crinoline while hairdressers sprinkled talcum powder all over her hair. This was her first big runway show in Paris, in the Louvre's Cour Carrée. She was sixteen, with a bony teenage body that would earn her the nicknames "The Twig" and "The Shrimp," and at 5'7" seemed short compared to the supermodels swirling around and towering over her, Naomi Campbell, Linda Evangelista, and Christy Turlington.

Everything seemed out of reach, beyond measure: "I had to come down the catwalk by myself. It looked huge, like an airport runway."[45] John Galliano's 1990 spring/summer collection was inspired by the flight of Czar Nicholas II's middle daughter, Anastasia. Galliano's only direction before Moss got onto the runway was: "Okay, Kate, you are being pursued by wolves." And a disciplined Kate followed the direction to the letter: defying convention, "She ran flat out," Galliano would recall. "Nobody had ever seen a crinoline flying like that on the catwalk! It was completely disrespectful. And everyone rose. It was a magic moment."[46]

The breaking out of Kate Moss was like an apparition. "In spite of the superb giantesses who were walking this runway, you were sort of hypnotized by her," recalled Sarah Doukas. "She may have been four inches shorter than the other models, but you only had eyes for her."[47] Moss's cheeky performance suddenly made the sameness of leggy runway

shows and their precisely timed hip swaying seem old. She was taking runway shows away from a parade of draped bodies and into something other, something unknown.

A birdlike face, a streamlined body: an Unidentified Flying Object had entered the decade.

A Chameleon Beauty

What did Moss have that her peers did not? How was she so different? How might one account for the fact that, with her first runway show, a model with such atypical measurements, so young and lacking in assurance, would be able to reach the level of supermodels such as Naomi Campbell, Linda Evangelista, and Claudia Schiffer? And what about the fact that she would later overshadow these models and become a genuine star whose look would be imitated the world over, a global brand and, perhaps, a myth? On the subject of Kate Moss, questions abound and opinions differ—the sign of a legend fed by enigmas, not feats.

One can scrutinize Moss's features with the attention of cosmetic surgeons who find perfection in the proportion of a face, the distance between the eyes, and the relationship between the base of the nose and the size of the lips, but the exercise leads nowhere. "A beauty without a hitch, worn naturally, and with the instinct of a 'chameleon'—such is

50

Kate Moss's definition of what a great model is," writes Françoise-Marie Santucci.[48]

Kate Moss was being pursued by wolves. But who were they? The wolves of masks that traffic in the notion of a problematic identity or the wolves of fables expressing a devouring fantasy that will be in effect in the great controversy of 1993, when Moss would be accused of promoting anorexia in young girls? Was she truly being pursued by wolves, or was she, instead, running to meet the wolves sitting on either side of the runway, the photographers now shooting her, the journalists who would pursue her for years to come?

With overly long teeth, bandy legs, and a face covered in freckles, Kate Moss immediately embodied a new look. Marketers had been trying to capture that look to seduce youth in the late 1980s, and advertisers would try to summon it by multiplying the use of oxymorons throughout the 1990s: transgression as norm, the rebel as "in," glamour in the streets, identity as a mix, modernity steeped in vintage, diversity as a label. As consumer researchers Yankelovich Partners put it in 1997, "Diversity is the key fact of life for Xers, the core of the perspective they bring to the marketplace. Diversity in all its forms—cultural, political, sexual, racial, social."[49]

But was this only about democratizing fashion in post-Thatcher England? Or was it about using a new image of glamour to capture the new youth market, by seeking what was "cool" in suburbs, schools, and coffee shops? Might Kate Moss have been the equivalent of the Nike marketing guys planted in inner cities to test products among targeted populations? The tactic is known as "bro-ing," coming from the expression: "Hey, bro! Check out the shoes!"[50]

Was Moss an expat of the suburbs like her friends Corinne Day, Melanie Ward, Mario Sorrenti, and John Galliano—who went to college in Croydon and whose father was a plumber? For photographer Nick Knight, who shot Moss for some ten *Vogue* covers, "There is a normalcy about her. She's very beautiful, of course…but she comes from the same world as I do. She's trendy, she's cool, she's funny, but in the end she's a young British girl like the others. Most models are much more difficult to pin down. You look at them and you never really know whether they come from Latvia, Miami, or someplace else."[51] David Bailey, the 1960s photographer who served as an inspiration for the photographer, Thomas, in Michelangelo Antonioni's *Blow-Up*, attributed Moss's success to her "totally democratic"[52] look:

"She's not too scary, she's practically within your reach. The kind of girl you would like as your next-door neighbor, except she'll never be your next-door neighbor."[53]

Open-Space Buddhism

One of the mysteries kept alive by the spontaneous ideology of fashion is its relationship to time. Expressions such as "the mood of the times," "the spirit of the times," "the atmosphere," or "the climate of the period" serve as so many useful crutches to evoke fashion's relationship to time without explaining it. This very characteristic allows fashion to entrust clothes and models with the role of interpreter or spokesperson for a period or generation without really clarifying the reasons for this mysterious affinity.

In Kate Moss's case, formulas expressing this collusion abound. She is "the face of an epoch," "the symbol of Generation X," "the figurehead of grunge," "the icon of cool." She embodies or symbolizes. She expresses or interprets. One is once again in a theater of representation that denies subjects and groups the possibility of having experiences or struggles. "Don't interpret! Experiment!" French philosopher Gilles Deleuze used to say. Together with the photographers, designers, and art directors who made her their figurehead in the early 1990s, Kate Moss should be credited with the power of experimentation.

The early Kate Moss was not an isolated phenomenon. At the time, she was one of thousands of teenagers running to castings, getting their pictures taken by their boyfriends, and dropping off a few shots at modeling agencies—in her case, the photo was a blurry Polaroid. Many doors were closed to Moss because of her small size and juvenile appearance, and her castings resulted in many disappointments. One could do better in terms of a flying start. For two years at least, Moss spent much time in suburban trains, running from one casting to the next without much result.

Fortunately, Corinne Day was there. Yet the Moss-Day sessions in a London suburb felt more like girlfriends' outings, where the two had fun taking photographs of themselves, than like professional shoots. Presented ten years earlier, the photographs eventually published in *The Face* would have remained at the bottom of a drawer, or at Mrs. Linda Moss's home in Croydon. Sarah Doukas's agency, Storm, "discovered" Moss, yet the company's name might appear somewhat self-important, given that it

Opposite, from left to right: Moss, Christy Turlington, and Naomi Campbell in floral dresses on the Isaac Mizrahi runway, November 1993.

53

represented only a handful of girls and all it was able to offer Moss was a teen magazine shoot. Far from the anti-model she would later be depicted as being, Moss was just a teen trying her luck without much hope, all the while annoying her mother, a woman with solid practical sense who did not believe in miracles.

There were many repentant former models around Moss, people who had given up and tried the other side of the camera, photographers like her boyfriend Mario Sorrenti and Corinne Day; like Sarah Doukas, who became her booker; or even like Paul Rowland, who had just opened his modeling agency—an office, really, not much more than a phone number on a business card—when Moss landed in New York in 1992. Rowland's Women Management agency may not have represented any models yet, but Rowland didn't lack for self-confidence: "The way my life works is things just come. I can never tell you what tomorrow is. I keep everything open. I keep everything moving and fluid. The thing that works for me is, I'm not afraid to attempt it."[54] It was an open-space form of Buddhism used as a marketing strategy. The idea might have seemed lightweight as Rowland was about to enter the American market, but this was early 1990, and this "Mr. Cool" was in sync with the times' ideology of spontaneity.

British Invasion

Change was not limited to Kate's look. A group of young people was about to accede to power in fashion, creating their own modeling agencies, taking over prestigious fashion magazines or couture houses in an irreverent mood. This group would not have made a fortune with alternative magazines like *The Face* and *i-D* anymore, but did with *Vogue*, *Harper's Bazaar*, *Elle*, and *Vanity Fair*. Hundred of covers and editorial fashion stories would soon carry the thousand-and-one faces of Kate Moss, while the tabloids would recount the daily travails of her tumultuous life.

Before becoming the figurehead of a generation, the diminutive Moss was that of a group of stylists and designers about to make their mark in haute couture, on runways, and with the critics. There would have been no Kate without those closest to her: Corinne Day, John Galliano, and Sarah Doukas. The new stylists and designers were a bunch of suburban kids—Melanie Ward; John Galliano, who attended the prestigious Saint Martins College of Art and Design and joined Christian Dior in 1992; Alexander McQueen, who joined Givenchy after attending Saint Martins as well; Mario Sorrenti, who would become Moss's boyfriend, photographer, and mentor, and whose mother, herself a fashion photographer, would chaperone and coach Moss in New York. All shared the intuition that an era was ending. Yet how many had had that same intuition before without ever finding their place in the new times? How might one, for instance, give proper credit to Corinne Day's brand of radicalism, which in other times would have been deemed naïve or regarded as incompetence?

The couture houses—Yves Saint Laurent, Christian Dior, Givenchy, Calvin Klein—would soon open their doors to this group. Prestigious magazines would change hands soon, too. This Anglo-Saxon wave, which people would even refer to as a British Invasion, would spread from London to Paris to New York City. Others would join in, such as Frenchman Fabien Baron, who had been at the helm of Italian *Vogue* in the 1980s and in 1990 became the artistic director of

Opposite: Gucci ready-to-wear, Spring/Summer 1995.

Above, left: Calvin Klein ready-to-wear, Spring/Summer 1996. Above, right: Calvin Klein ready-to-wear, Fall/Winter 1996–97.

Interview, the magazine founded by Andy Warhol. Hired as artistic director to give the dated *Harper's Bazaar* a new look in 1992, Baron had barely started when photographs of Kate Moss invaded the magazine's pages. Later, as a consultant for Calvin Klein, Baron would make Moss the label's figurehead. A few years later, when the old Burberry brand needed some dusting off to suit current tastes and adapt to Tony Blair's "Cool Britannia" campaign, the Baron-Moss team would be in command once again.

In 1992, former British *Vogue* editor Liz Tilberis took over as editor-in-chief of *Harper's Bazaar*. Beginning with her first issue in September 1992, she stated her ambitions: "The best of the best, in every field!" Tilberis sought elegance of spirit as much as of appearance. "An identity that's well-balanced yet centered." That was a bit cryptic. And above all, given the economic crisis, she emphasized new shapes, new moods, and new styles. Certainly, the program was a bit vague. But a fashion magazine isn't a political party: it demonstrates movement by moving forward. In this respect, *Harper's Bazaar*'s table of contents constituted a generational manifesto, with articles about Ariane Mnouchkine's "total theater" and Paul Auster's novels, as well as Kate Moss's first editorial fashion story in the magazine, shot by Patrick Demarchelier, titled "Wild: Fashion Breaks the Rules." This story also marked the first time Moss worked with Demarchelier. About ten more editorial fashion stories would follow, all of them produced by the Baron-Moss-Demarchelier trio.

Throughout the decade, Baron would establish himself as a fashion and visual-communication guru, called to the deathbeds of labels in search of identity. Armani, Balenciaga, Hugo Boss, Prada, Valentino, and Burberry were reborn under his influence. His remedy was simple and infallible: "Modernizing the brand without losing its history." In this respect, Moss was a substantial ally: chameleon and trans-formist, she was a vehicle of stories and fictions, an actress more than a model. Their team would work miracles, to the big brands' greatest fortune.

Fashion-conscious in the Suburbs

Within fashion's tightly closed world, Moss—like Twiggy—was one of the rare models to embrace her modest origins, going so far as to use them as the basis of her legend and vocation. "I was just like my friends in Croydon…. They were fashion-conscious because they were suburban, and that's the way suburban people are. They're more fashion-conscious and they're more trendy."[55] For Moss and her friends, fashion was neither a frivolous subject nor mere affectation nor typical fin-de-siècle dandyism. Its stakes went far beyond the style or look favored by marketers; as surprising as it may seem, fashion to them also included a question of consciousness.

Moss explained that when one was young and living in a London suburb, one was fashion-conscious. Choosing a garment, a pair of boots, or a jacket wasn't just a question of taste. The choice also had a strategic stake: it was a visa used to cross social boundaries, a sign of identity. Fakes and discounted pieces were not a possibility. A lapse or near-lapse in taste resulted in social exclusion, in being labeled a zero or tacky. One had to be cool, trendy, or fun—a word that recurred frequently in Moss's interviews—or become invisible. Suburban kids wanted to be seen, whether it was on runways, in

stadiums, on stages, on screens, or in the streets. Rap music was constantly making this very same complaint. Sports marketing would turn rap into an epic—that of the visible body, of its arrival and its takeoff, of its speed and its victory. MTV would be its mirror.

This new "fashion consciousness" revealed the extreme importance of fashion in processes of legitimization, to the point where it became a question of social survival for individuals facing exclusion or marginalization. Sailor, the friendly, romantic protagonist of David Lynch's *Wild at Heart*, was basically saying as much when he claimed emphatically that his snakeskin jacket (which he was never without) was the "symbol of [his] individuality and [his] belief in personal freedom." He was a Don Quixote of grunge, as were all Generation Xers. In the final analysis, they fell victims to the same sort of misconception as the sad-faced knight who had taken a colander for a knight's helmet and made

60

use of garments not for what they were—mere objects of consumption—but as experiences to be lived, vehicles for a more novelistic life.

It is, of course, possible to deride the fact that brands have taken such importance in the suburbs of the Western world, where some men (as Naomi Klein recounts) love their sneakers more than their girlfriends.[56] Yet such derision would fail to understand the role brands play in a social economy where each person is led to making strategic use of himself to maximize his value. This entails producing and controlling one's life, which is viewed as an uninterrupted performance worth only as much as the effect it has on others. Seen under this angle, suburban teens are not "alienated" by consumer society, as is often said. Rather, they are extremely aware of the logics of ranking and distinction at work in fashion.

What's the Story?

From 1988 to 1992, Kate Moss made gradual inroads into the fashion-week circuit, becoming a regular at the presentations in New York, Paris, and Milan. During this period, she devoted most of her time to editorial fashion stories in trendy magazines, finding willing accomplices in the best fashion photographers, who loved Moss because she excelled in role playing. Rather than selling clothes, a fashion story features a model inhabiting a setting. The work doesn't always pay well, but it is an essential part of establishing a figure that is able to embody all roles. Fashion stories are a model's academy. And during this training period, Kate the Shrimp, as finely wrought as the first letter in a magazine article, would reveal herself to be most gifted.

Evidence of this lies in the pages of *Harper's Bazaar* and *Vogue* in the early 1990s, where Moss unveiled the chameleon personality that would become her own brand. According to Véronique Rampazzo of the Marilyn Agency, "It is precisely because Kate Moss has 'easy' features and nothing special or striking that it is easy for her to transform herself, to interpret: she is imminently malleable."[57] Years later, every person who ever worked with Moss would still remember her extraordinary talent. Among them was designer Stefano Gabbana: "Kate is more of an actress than a model," he said. "She is able to interpret many kinds of woman. She was on the catwalks of many of our fashion shows throughout the 1990s."[58] According to photographer Willy Vanderperre, "She is completely focused, completely available, she gives a lot of herself." In 2005, Vanderperre transformed Moss into a hat- and tie-wearing androgynous icon for *Another Man* magazine.[59] "For my spring/summer 2008 campaign, I wanted a woman, someone who could tell a story," explained designer Donna Karan. "Kate has that depth of experience."[60]

When Moss recalled her runway shows for John Galliano, she spoke as an actress would: "It was amazing, like a high.... John tells you your character and you just get so into it because of the energy."[61] And regardless of who the photographer or the designer was for whom she was posing or walking, Moss would make it a habit to ask before each session: "What's the story?" "I don't like doing pictures as myself," she told *Interview*. "I like to be made into somebody different. In a picture, it's hard to be yourself. But when you're pretending to be someone else, it's nice. It's fun. It's more interesting."[62]

Kate Moss is a purveyor of composite looks, a fashion deejay who mixes identities, habits, and periods. Some collect Old Masters and other artworks; she cultivates hybridization: her savage shopping practices—buying at flea markets, from antique dealers, from costume designers—allowed her to build an imaginary museum of fashion, a collection of images and fantasies from which she drew, blending decades in the process. Moss continued this practice past the grunge years, eventually turning it into a label. A regular customer at Steinberg & Tolkien, London's vintage mecca, Moss could fall in love with such historic pieces as "a costume from the Folies Bergères, a beaded Basque-waisted can-can skirt with a hat trimmed in marabou with a champagne glass on top," said director Tracey Tolkien. "I think she was thinking, 'I don't know where I'll wear it.' But she was really just enjoying it, letting her imagination run wild. I think you have to want to imagine the person who wore it and the adventures they had in it; you have to have that romantic attitude towards it."[63]

In Moss's eyes, clothes are, above all, signs with which she plays. People say she is photogenic, but she is mostly a semiophile: a warrior with a smooth body, she makes signs and habitus dance. "So Kate," people say to describe her—a tautological definition that perpetuates the mystery, or the paradox, of a chameleon identity that allows Moss to change her appearance without ceasing to be recognizable. "The woman of fashion dream[s] of being at once herself

Above: Guy Laroche Haute Couture,
Fall/Winter 1996–97. **Pages 64–65,
from left to right:** Jil Sander ready-
to-wear, Spring/Summer 1995;
Versace Haute Couture, Spring/
Summer 1993; Versace ready-
to-wear, Spring/Summer 1995;
Salvatore Ferragamo ready-to-wear,
Spring/Summer 1995.

and another," Roland Barthes wrote in 1967, adding:
"The multiplication of persons in a single being is always
considered by Fashion as an index of power.... It is the final
luxury of a person rich enough to be multiplied, stable enough
never to be lost; thus we see Fashion 'play' with the most
serious theme of human conscience (Who am I?)."[64]

In the 1990s, however, a chameleon personality
represented much more than a sign within a semiotic
system similar to the one Barthes established in *The
Fashion System*: Moss had become the ideal type for a
society that was, according to former model Patrícia Soley-
Beltran, seeking "subjects who were able to constantly
acquire new skills, social mobility, and malleability in order
to adapt to a highly volatile labor market."[65] Therefore, the
craze provoked by Kate Moss's irruption went well beyond
the mere curiosity arising from a new model's arrival on the
scene or from the excitement following the unveiling of a
new collection. It was the curtain call of a new era.

The Symbol of Liquid Modernity

The years to come were to be "active, "technological," "vigorous," and "happy," the French magazine *Actuel* predicted as the 1980s began. "We want to tell modern adventures, and tell stories minute by minute. Report on the latest technologies transforming our lives. Talk about today's emotions. Give you the raw elements of reality." Ten years later, a new subject came to life, who was neither vigorous, nor happy, nor even active, but rather "uncertain," "precarious," "flexible," and even "liquid." The taste for the real would give birth to reality television, and the passion for storytelling would be contained and diverted by new narrative machines serving corporations and public relations agencies as well as political and military organizations.

Thus a new language emerged, which borrowed from the lexicons of fashion and management, turning fashion away from its function as spectacle or object of contemplation and into performance. Its key words were "agility" and "leanness." A new aesthetic was imposed on management, and, in the words of sociologist Richard Sennett, corporations were called upon to "look beautiful in the eyes of the passing voyeur"[66] (that is, pension funds and financial investors) by showing themselves to be capable of reform and layoffs. Hiring workers ceased to be a sign of economic health, becoming instead synonymous with poor management and bureaucracy; layoffs now brought value to a corporation and boosted its stock.

Managerial "beauty" bore the signs of flexibility and change. Fashion recognized those signs and adopted them. On the management side, this trend yielded the type of "lean management" adopted by Toyota in Japan and theorized by M.I.T. in the 1980s. On the fashion side, the invention of a "fashion body," which Karl Lagerfeld defined as "a silhouette made out of a mold, extraordinarily narrow, with never-ending arms and legs, a very long neck, and a very small head. You can't have large bones. Some things cannot be made any thinner." It was as if the "new economy," management, cultural industries, and news and communication technologies had met up to invent a new person at the turn of the twenty-first century.

According to Richard Sennett, the culture of this new capitalism needed "[a] new self, oriented to the short term, focused on potential ability, willing to abandon past experience."[67] Like all revolutions, the neoliberal revolution demanded a profound overhaul of the ideals that inspired or legitimized behaviors. In her trenchant manner, British prime minister Margaret Thatcher had defined its purpose as early as 1988: "The economy is but a tool. The goal is to change souls."[68]

"What values and practices can hold people together," Richard Sennett asked, "as the institutions in which they live fragment?… How to manage short-term relationships, and oneself, while migrating from task to task … How to develop new skills?… Most people are not like this," he added, "they take pride in being good at something specific, and they value the experiences they have lived." And above all, he wrote, "they need a sustaining life narrative."[69]

How was one to make them change their minds? The answer lay in Sennett's last remark: if people's need for a sustaining life narrative could no longer be satisfied, they would subscribe to new narratives that would make a hero out of a flexible self, a self that was liberated from the long term and open to any and all metamorphoses. This idea would become a theory in 2000, with sociologist Zygmunt Bauman's concept of "liquid modernity."[70] Virtue could no longer reside in conformity to rules—which, in any case, are rare and contradictory—but in flexibility: the ability to rapidly change tactics and styles, to abandon commitment and loyalties without regret, and to take advantage of opportunities according to one's personal preferences. As a result, the challenge no longer consisted in "remaining true to oneself" in a changing environment but rather in changing constantly and adapting to life's fluctuating circumstances. As long as it also seemed to be a cultural fact, a new fashion, or a novel, this obligation was likely to be accepted as economic necessity.

This was a revolution the likes of which occur only once or twice in a century—a new disposition between the political and the technological, economy and culture, fashion and communication. Kate Moss was the child of this encounter. Some of those who knew her during these years stressed her instinctive, unfinished style. For photographer Bruce Weber, "The excitement you feel when photographing her can only be compared to what you feel when photographing an animal that's just born, or a little wild kid."[71] It was as if we were witnessing the creation of a prototype, at once style, lifestyle, and model—the software of an era. Kate Moss was a figure of the postindustrial edge.

Thus, the heroine of Burberry and Tony Blair's "Cool Britannia" appeared as a creation of the biopolitical age, which not only tamed bodies but also endeavored to delineate experiences and inspire roles and behaviors. It was no longer sufficient to simply dress silhouettes; now one had to define possible behaviors and give life to characters. With Moss, the "fashion body" ceased to be a support for the garment; it was written, encoded, programmed. An object of worship? A model to be imitated? Above all, an inspiring narrative.

The Kate Moss "legend" draws on a bible of characters who build and disseminate the ideal types of the new era and outline the behavior of the new subject. Moss's nickname "The Twig" is eloquent in this respect: she is modeling flexibility and transformism within a value system that substitutes a mobile, even mutant ideal (the beautiful is in what changes, adapts, restructures itself) for the traditional aesthetic ideal (the beautiful is in what lasts). Blasé irony, typical whybotherism, and blatant anticonformism—all Generation X features that Kate Moss recycles in her own fashion—make up the distinctive signs of a distancing from any sort of model. This is what makes the phenomenon so paradoxical and elusive. If fashion's role is to provide models for identification, Kate Moss is the anti-model: she represents indifference toward codes, anticonformism, and a refusal to imitate—a modeling oxymoron. A kind of runway puppet who has embraced the motto: "Walk the walk, but don't talk the talk."

From then on, fashion as a business field would dissolve into popular subculture. Haute couture (an array of rare objects with high added value and differentiating power) and ready-to-wear weren't fashion's exclusive objects anymore. Fashion now included a much larger field than the mere garment: it included life. Furthermore, fashion no longer designed styles for clothes only; it now designed modes of subjection—in other words, a lifestyle. Its goal became the transformation of daily life into an exclusive zone of valorization and commercial exchanges.

Fashion as a collection of signs and styles disappeared in favor of fashion as a social laboratory, where new relationships to the body and to desire, along with the ephemeral and nomadic character of any activity and creation, were objects of experimentation. Fashion became the key segment in a new array of business fields that might be characterized as "the cosmetics-industrial complex," whose aim was no longer just to entertain or to show, but rather to "coach" individuals in the broadest possible sense. This was accomplished through a network of consultants and human-capital experts whose mission was to convince individuals to make strategic use of themselves. As repeated by a long string of celebrities, the L'Oréal slogan "Because I'm Worth It" represented the pithy expression of this new culture of performance. Value had lost all referent; now the proof of its value lay in asserting itself as value.

Consequently, it wasn't fashion that converted to realism at the dawn of the 1990s, it was the entire social reality, which became an object of fashion—fashionable. Life ceased to appear solely as what had to be lived (a place of experiences) and turned into a space for experimentation and the strategic use of the self, with each individual becoming an object to be styled, made over, and coached. The goal of fashion no longer consisted of adorning the body, clothing it, and embellishing it; its aim was to convince us that, in a person's life, everything had become an object of fashion—fashionable.

As a result, "fashion consciousness" played the same role as moral conscience and political conscience in political democracies (or religious conscience in theocratic nations): fashion took the shape of an immediate and intuitive knowledge of norms and ideal types that inspired social behaviors in a "fashion society" where the value of individuals now lay exclusively in their ability to have the right look at the right time.

Casting became the rule, and the street became a source of inspiration for runway performances presented as life itself. Supermodels were no longer its heroines, "ordinary persons" were—individuals as masters and owners of their styles, as lords and designers of themselves. Fashion fused with mass culture and began to live according to the rhythm of its debates and scandals. What was until then a mere cliché propagated by Chanel's mythology became a reality: fashion was taking to the streets, where it joined the carnival-like parade, now in motion, that included retinues of disheveled nymphets, unhinged stars, and figureheads of earlier decades from whom it borrowed costumes and masks, wigs, and hats. And Kate Moss was its idol.

3

WILD AT HEART

HERE IS THE FIGURE OF THE MODEL
as described by Roland Barthes in the late 1960s: "She has
no knowledge of evil, to any degree whatsoever. For, not
having to deal with her defects and difficulties, Fashion never
speaks of love, it knows neither adultery nor affairs nor even
flirtation: in Fashion, a woman always travels with her
husband…. In this way, Fashion immerses the woman
about whom and to whom it speaks in a state of innocence,
where everything is for the best in the best of possible
worlds."[72] Ever since its late nineteenth-century invention
by the British-born French couturier Charles Frederick
Worth and Jeanne Paquin's first runway shows in early
twentieth-century Paris, the model existed in an ideal and
virtuous world "in which nothing happens," a universe
without pulse or history, shielded from the vicissitudes of
life, and according to Barthes, governed by a strange "law
of euphoria," which "forbids [Fashion] to offer anything
aesthetically or morally disgraceful."[73]

Page 70: A page from an editorial spread for *Allure* magazine, photographed by Frédérique Veysset at the Hotel Raphael, Paris, 1991. **Above, left:** Walking the runway for Alexander McQueen's first New York show, March 1996. **Above, right:** Vivienne Westwood ready-to-wear, Spring/Summer 1996. **Opposite:** Vivienne Westwood ready-to-wear, Fall/Winter 1994–95.

The Heroin Addict's Delight

At the beginning of the 1990s, fashion became unhinged and put the standards of glamour to a serious test. This was an upheaval of the canons of beauty and the moral principles that had framed fashion until that time. The "law of euphoria" ceased to apply. Not only had sex and venial sins ("adultery," "affairs," and "flirtation") invaded fashion, but anorexia and drugs were now threatening teenagers' health and lives.

This change was so brutal that it failed to be perceived by many fashion observers. Such was the case with French sociologist Gilles Lipovetsky who, in his 1997 essay titled "The Third Woman," continued to describe fashion in Barthes's terms, as a "euphoric culture of beauty, where ambivalence and unhealthy, deathly negativism are expunged."[74] He wrote:

"In the terminal stages of beauty, feminine charms are no longer associated with the fall and death, but with celebrity, happiness, and fortune." On the subject of models, Lipovetsky added that it was "impossible to find anything depraved or destructive." Impossible, really, when Kate Moss's escapades had been making headlines for the last seven years?

That same year, on May 7, 1997, United States president Bill Clinton made a solemn declaration following the death from an over-dose of Davide Sorrenti, Mario's brother: "The glorification of heroin is not creative, it's destructive. It's not beautiful, it's ugly. This is not about art. It's about life and death. And glorifying death is not good for any society."[75] Precisely one year before, on May 7, 1996, *New York Times* fashion critic Amy Spindler had claimed that the 1990s would go down in history as "the decade when fashion served as a pusher—a pusher of what appears to be the best-dressed heroin addicts in history."[76] Denouncing the decade's "decadent look" as illustrated by the successive figures of grunge, waifs, and heroin addicts, she observed: "Other fashion references have faded away…[but the] heroin-addict look…has had the tenacity in fashion of, well, an addiction."

Opposite, clockwise from top left: Missoni ready-to-wear, Fall/Winter 1996–97; Versace Haute Couture, Spring/Summer 1996; Chloé ready-to-wear, Fall/Winter 1995–96.

Fashion without History

Fashion may have been the twentieth century's first manifestation of a social universe governed by its own logic—like the "financial bubble" and the "Internet bubble" later—and shielded from any disturbance from the real. No political or social event ever had any grip on it. Fashion seemed to be saying the more things change, the more things remain the same. It would do whatever it fancied and answer only to its own whims, all the while initiating imperceptible changes noticed only after the fact, in news photos or family albums, where this outdated hairstyle, that overly long or overly short skirt, these oversized shoulder pads, or those very high-waisted pants would come as a surprise.

Until the 1990s, the fashion bubble developed in an entirely autonomous manner within an independent social universe and against the grain of mass culture (films, photo-stories, romances, working-class newspapers), whose narratives were usually dramatic, even catastrophic. Contrary to this bad-fortune pathos, fashion exhibited an ideal world, free of contradictions. The female model can be said to have represented its promise, or its proof, a ghost from the paradise of concordances and harmonies, the divine boutique

74

Above, left: Versace Haute Couture, Fall/Winter 1996–97. Above, right: Vivienne Westwood ready-to-wear, Spring/Summer 1995.

where everything suits you. France's privileged witness to this immutable world, the charming and antiquated magazine *Petit Echo de la Mode* (founded in 1880 and closed in 1983), was entirely devoted to positive values and seemingly immune to disturbances such as the evolution of mores and the horrors of two world wars. It would document this flat world, free of intrigue or temporality, for an entire century.

Before the 1990s, and contrary to film actresses, the female model had no history. She resolutely kept her distance from the political sphere. At the time, nothing was more improbable than a model paying a visit to a head of state, as Kate Moss and Naomi Campbell did with Fidel Castro in 1998. The Cuban leader felt so honored by this visit that he promptly granted them the status of "revolutionaries" because one was a short and the other a black top model.

Kept at a distance from history and politics, female models knew neither the temptation of evil nor the anguish of desire. They were smooth, matte surfaces on which garments came into relief. If fashion itself knew seasonal inflections, its pat models remained remarkably unperturbed. They appeared and disappeared according to the rhythm of photo shoots and runway shows, like nuns faithfully attending every church service. Models belonged to the endlessly repeated cult that fashion paid to the god of style, in which they were merely officiating. Garments were what models gave life to, which implied that they themselves vanished, along with the signs of their own lives. Silhouettes walking the runways, models were the silent sentinels of fashion.

Models' commonality with nuns resided in the fact that they were both entirely devoted to a single cause, that they existed solely within and through a liturgy: while the former donned the veil and vowed to be obedient and chaste, the latter vowed allegiance to the garment. The models' physical expressions were codified in a rigorous, monastic ritual. They had to learn how to walk, adopt a certain way of carrying their heads, conform to a grammar of gestures. This was an entire orthopedics, according to Michel Foucault, that saw the organization of convents as a model for a disciplinary society.[77] Contrary to the discipline of nuns, that of fashion did not, however, aim to enslave or recruit, but rather to celebrate: fashion was a convent devoted to the invocation of beautiful style. It certainly had its rules, liturgies, and officiating priestesses, but the indispensable discipline in this cult represented one element of a stylistics of the body rather than an orthopedics: it made sure that singular features, faults, and disproportions were erased; it sought to regulate forms of appearance, movements, and sequences; it was less interested in taming the body than in sublimating it in a ritual whose final purpose was to let the garment speak.

This type of fashion paid homage to the couturier's genius and also celebrated the modest virtues of well-crafted work. It claimed an ethic as much as it did aesthetics: praising the atelier assistants, taking pride in a savoir-faire handed down through generations, fashion kept alive a sort of guild for seamstresses, those noncommissioned officers who formed the largest contingent of the battalions of beauty. Mutual aid. Humility. Perseverance. The seamstresses sewed, embroidered, and restitched while cultivating a form of integrity that turned into heroism when their vision failed, arthritis attacked their deformed hands, and their backs became hunched. Weren't novices initiated to this kind of work upon entering a convent? Might fashion be the antechamber of sainthood? Models were in the same boat as seamstresses. In any case, they were expected to show the same self-effacement. Weren't models extensions of the altar or the cutting table during fittings?

The Novel of Fashion

Why was traditional fashion so alien from what Barthes used to call "the infernal regions of desire"? These were the regions in which both the heroines of popular novels and Hollywood actresses were born and delighted, and which literature has explored, from Samuel Richardson's first novels to those of Virginia Woolf, through Pierre Choderlos de Laclos's *Dangerous Liaisons*, the Marquis de Sade's works, Gustave Flaubert's *Madame Bovary*, and Leo Tolstoy's *Anna Karenina*, to cite only a few of the most famous examples. Was it because of its proximity to desire and seduction that for such a long time fashion erected around itself, as around a convent, impassible barriers designed to keep it from coming into contact with evil?

According to Barthes, fashion's exception was a function of the law of nonwritten euphoria that characterizes literature aimed at young girls, which blended with "the language of a mother who 'preserves' her daughter from all contact with evil."[78] This exception was all the more remarkable, Barthes noted, given that "Fashion rhetoric tends increasingly to the novelistic." How, then, might one imagine a novel from which evil is absent, "a continuously euphoric novel"? The rise of the *nouveau roman*, which at the time was finding its way outside the well-beaten path of intrigue, may have led Barthes to imagine this sort of anti-novel of fashion, a "rudimentary, formless novel without temporality."[79] But Barthes could have given up this improbable novel just as easily and chosen to locate his "language of fashion" next to non-narrative physical disciplines such as ballet, dancing, and gymnastics. For Barthes, the reason was that he was searching for a compromise between what he had identified as fashion's law of euphoria and what, just before the events of May 1968, he perceived as an inescapable evolution of fashion, which "tends increasingly to the novelistic."

For Barthes, the difficulty was not limited to his method—that is, a semiotic system he said was the result of a sort of scientific euphoria. Like any thinker, Barthes was locked in his own late-1960s horizon. In short, he was ahead of his subject. And it was precisely at the point, where the semiotic system he had conceived ran counter to his own intuition of the contradictions undermining fashion's universe in the late 1960s, that Barthes pointed to the road ahead. For it was only after the fall of the Berlin Wall more than twenty years later, in the contradictory situation created by the "narrative impasse" evoked in the first chapter of this book, that fashion's antihistorical universe exploded under the impact of "the new narrative order" that was beginning to structure the way in which the globalized cultural industry functioned.[80] In 1993, the historical logic that prompted fashion to embrace mass culture's narrative schematics would blow its previous timeless logic to smithereens. And from this "Big Bang" fashion emerged utterly transformed.

From this moment on, fashion would no longer immerse women in an "innocent state," but rather in a worldly inferno where the signs of beauty were associated with the stigmas of extreme emaciation and drugs. Against a background of overdoses and news items relating the deaths from exhaustion of undernourished models, the debate that had been brewing since the beginning of the 1990s broke into the open, with Kate Moss at its epicenter.

In the Eye of the Cyclone

The year 1993 marked the end of Kate Moss's mutation. Now on the cover of the biggest magazines, Moss was no longer a mere inspiration for fashion's new trends; she gave rise to controversies and societal debates. Calvin Klein's figurehead was everywhere—in the streets, on the sides of buses, at bus stops, all over TV screens and magazine covers. Her frail silhouette had become a social topic. At nineteen, she was the stake of colossal financial calculations, brand strategies, and aesthetic and moral challenges she could not grasp. Champagne and tobacco—to mention only her official pharmacopeia—helped to keep her going. Her name was synonymous with several scandals. Because of Moss, columnists became indignant and doctors who worried about her influence on teenage health issued severe warnings. As previously noted, her style was a subject of concern that, a few years later, would even extend to the Oval Office.

Two scandals took place within a few weeks. A fashion story titled "Underexposure," published in the May 1993 issue of British *Vogue*, provoked the first one. The editorial consisted of eight pages of photographs of Kate Moss shot by Corinne Day. Moss was wearing lingerie, which triggered mass indignation. The photographer was reproached for aestheticizing junkies and worse, trafficking in the eroticization of children. The British daily the *Independent* reproached *Vogue* for its "irresponsibility" in choosing pictures that were evocative of the sexualization of children. For her part, *Cosmopolitan* editor-in-chief Marcelle D'Argy Smith deemed the photographs "hideous and tragic.... If I had a daughter who looked like that, I would take her to see a doctor." At stake here was the waif look, "a man's fantasy of shrinking women down to a manageable size," said Susan Faludi, author of the renowned 1991 *Backlash: The Undeclared War Against American Women*, in an interview for *People* magazine. "The look is about being very weak and passive. It's a very Victorian portrait of a woman where you are so weak you can barely get off your chaise longue and on to the retirement home."[81] Fueled by the tabloids, the scandal, the wrath of feminists, and the concern of therapists all came at a felicitous moment for the fashion industry, which saw grunge as the ruin of glamour and, by extension, as its own demise. Kate Moss stood in the eye of the cyclone. In fall 1993, the controversy

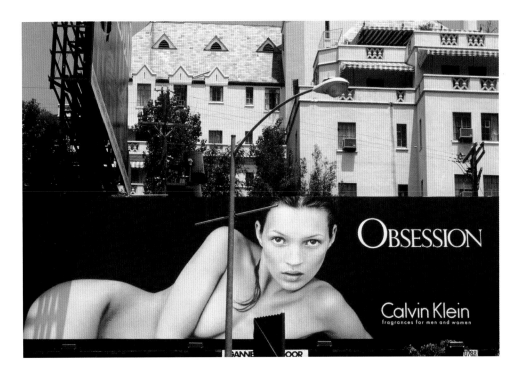

Opposite: A defaced Calvin Klein bus advertisement featuring Moss, 1994. At the time, many people accused Moss of encouraging anorexia through displays of her thin figure. **Above:** A Calvin Klein billboard advertisement for Obsession on Sunset Boulevard, Los Angeles, 1995.

initiated by Corinne Day's *Vogue* photographs doubled in scope with the launch of Calvin Klein's Obsession perfume campaign. This time around, Moss was not at fault for looking like an abandoned child or a junkie but for her excessive emaciation, which was perceived as encouraging anorexia. *Esquire* magazine published a fake ad ("Feed The Waifs") that included a picture of Moss and a very special offer: "For just 39 cents a day, less than the cost of a cup of coffee, you can keep this girl, and other supermodels just like her, alive."[82]

In the United States feminists plastered the slogans "Feed Me!" "Give Me a Cheeseburger!" and "Anorexia" over bus advertisements featuring a naked, reclining Moss. MediaWatch, a consumer activist organization, was critical of "images of women who are both naked and look hurt."[83] *People* magazine devoted its cover to Moss, unambiguously titling the issue "Skin & Bones." *People* turned to eating-disorders specialists for answers. The head of a clinic said she had taken in an anorexic girl who wanted to look like Kate Moss. Plastic surgeons claimed they had encountered patients brandishing Moss's photograph. In fact, being anorexic is not something everyone can achieve, as French psychiatrist Gérard Apfeldorfer remarked in the daily *Libération* in 2006: "There are psychological dispositions, family antecedents. In its most common form, this disease is the symptom of a narcissistic disorder, not of a desire to imitate models."[84]

Opposite: Jean Colonna ready-to-wear, Fall/Winter 1995–96. **Above, left:** Gucci ready-to-wear, Spring/ Summer 2000. **Above, right:** Chanel ready-to-wear, Spring/ Summer 1994.

How the Fashion Industry Killed the Street Urchin

The fact is that Kate Moss had quite a good appetite. When Benetton plastered city walls in Italy with the picture of a truly anorexic girl in 2007, the difference between her and Calvin Klein's Kate Moss was plain to see. The question then became: Why did such a cabal take place? The answer was to be found in a 1994 *New York Times* article entitled "How Fashion Killed the Unloved Waif."[85] "There was no Yalta summit of fashion's heads of state…." Amy Spindler wrote. "Magazine editors, certain designers and retail joined forces like characters in an Agatha Christie novel to deal a death blow to the waif."[86]

In truth, the haute couture industry did not have much taste for the waif's irruption on the podiums and in

83

magazines: while she did correspond to a certain state of mind for the youth of the day, she was no real help to sales and advertising budgets. The grunge look did not mean good business for magazines and advertising: "It wasn't working," declared *Vogue*'s Anna Wintour, in 1994, referring to the waif look. "The granny slip with sneakers is too difficult. And no makeup and dirty hair is not what the Leonard Lauders of this world want to see,"[87] referring to the then chief executive of the Estée Lauder Companies, a crucial advertiser for fashion magazines.

It was time to announce the return of glamour, and Anna Wintour took on that task, meeting with department-store fashion directors in March 1994 and declaring that *Vogue* "believed in one thing: glamour."[88] The word was out. *Harper's Bazaar*'s July 1994 cover proclaimed: "Shock Treatment." In May, *Vogue* had defined the new ideal as "Strong and Sexy." For a time, German model Nadja Auermann and her "steely femininity" took Kate the Shrimp's place on the cover of both magazines. Even though they had been the initiators of the waif look, Marc Jacobs and John Galliano introduced glamour in their collections for spring/summer 1994, as they had done with grunge before. In his runway show, Galliano introduced diamonds, a veritable totem in *Vogue*'s renewed conquest of glamour. As the designer most compromised by the waif look, Calvin Klein made amends and conformed to the industry's new guidelines.

In a pair of high heels, lips painted red, Kate Moss shelved away the languid poses of the Obsession campaign and adopted a style more in keeping with the codes of the moment. Sarah Doukas forbade her to work with Corinne Day, who, now in trouble with *Vogue*, temporarily left fashion to explore art and documentary photography. "The industry had pigeonholed her as the photographer of grunge," critic Hilton Als wrote in *The New Yorker*. "It took what it needed from her and moved on."[89]

Interpreting this turnaround as a simple return to the timeless canons of classic fashion as analyzed by Roland Barthes would be missing the point. At the time, the return of glamour was but a temporary retreat to the fundamentals of fashion. Because it partook of an irreversible mutation of our relationships to body, sex, and gender, the 1993 "Kate Moss Revolution" had in fact left deep marks.

For people just now discovering Corinne Day's work, the photographs published in *Vogue* in June 1993 do not appear dishonorable. Kate Moss was posing in her underwear in her London apartment, sitting on a radiator or leaning against a wall, surrounded by colored lights similar to those seen in shop windows at Christmas. A Lou Reed cassette lay on the floor, a clear allusion to the world of drugs, according to critics. Furnishings were kept to a minimum: a TV, a telephone, a chest of drawers, a stereo. Looking at these images years later, the strong reactions they provoked are somewhat baffling. At nineteen, Moss could in no way be mistaken for a twelve-year-old girl, as critics claimed at the time. Furthermore, Day's photographs were not erotic in any way: they showed a young woman just out of bed, or just about to get dressed to go out—the kind of images that have become banal on the Internet in the twenty-first century, ever since webcams started intruding on teenagers' privacy. Here, a seemingly chilly Kate was looking through the window while modestly pulling down her T-shirt. She seemed to be hesitating between going out and staying home, floating in a space between night and day, inside and out, adolescence and adulthood.

This may have represented a generational phenomenon, but it was first and foremost the illustration of a feeling of uncertainty in the face of history, a feeling that manifests itself time and time again when the future seems blocked. So it was between the two world wars, when Franz Kafka, stuck in his hometown of Prague, "this little mother with claws," suddenly wondered in his journal: "How does one inhabit?" The question served as an epigraph for films such as Gus Van Sant's *My Own Private Idaho* and *Last Days*. For "inhabiting" not only means occupying a space, but also finding a place in the social world. Wearing clothes, but also making habitus one's own, interiorizing acquired experience in the form of behavior codes.[90] A half century later, this vast question had become an equation for a generation that felt excluded from the social world, torn between hypermodernity and the return to a state of nature.

Indeed, what did the waif look consist of other than the mise-en-scène, or staging, of an abandoned street urchin who had gone back to a wild state? Coming to the fore once again in the early 1990s, the "return to the wild" was updating a number of themes that literature had exploited regularly since Daniel Defoe's 1719 *Robinson Crusoe*: the shipwreck, the breakdown of social ties, the struggle for survival, the encounter with the imposing Other (the savage, the indigenous being, the woman). The French literary critic Marthe Robert viewed what she called "Robinsonnades" as one of the places where the novel was born.[91] In the

1990s, films made the back-to-the-wild theme their own. David Lynch's *Wild at Heart*, for example, told the story of two lovers fleeing the young woman's mother and her murderous mobster friends, with the couple representing a world where sexual instincts and death wishes dominated. The title itself placed the movie under the sign of the world's return to the wild.

A worldwide publishing success in 1992, Clarissa Pinkola Estés's *Women Who Run with the Wolves*[92] was a popular anthology that included some of the universal myths and tales in which the woman figure reclaims her wild nature. According to the author, the wild woman was the victim of civilization; she had been hounded by society, which forced her to conform to the reductive mold of the roles she was assigned and kept her from hearing the generous voice from deep within her soul. Such was also the theme of director Ridley Scott's film *Thelma and Louise*, a lyrical ode to the wild woman.

In keeping with the times, *Harper's Bazaar* ran its first fashion story featuring Moss in fall 1992: "Wild, Fashion Breaks the Rules" was a transparent reference to Lou Reed's famous song, "Walk On The Wild Side." An ingenious designer and businessman, Calvin Klein, fifty at the time, went farther: by weaving together both waif and wild themes, he turned Kate Moss into the face of the "Wild Woman" myth.

Robinsonnades and Reality Television

Jost Van Dyke is a tiny part of the British Virgin Islands named after a Dutch pirate. The Barefoot Island is a port of call a few square miles wide, renowned among yacht owners for its relaxed lifestyle, its protected anchorages, its fine sand beaches, and its seaside bars. It is where, in 1993, Calvin Klein decided to parachute Kate Moss and her twenty-one-year-old boyfriend, Mario Sorrenti, charging him with photographing the next Obsession campaign. This was a tall order for Sorrenti, who was coming to this particular exercise after legendary photographers such as Richard Avedon as well as filmmaker David Lynch, who had shot the campaign the year before. Lynch did the only thing he knew how to do: shoot a movie, not an ad—and not what Klein was looking for. Later, the designer would explain that he had let himself be persuaded by the young Mario's journal, which was adorned with naked photos of Moss and poems dedicated to her: "It was perfect for Obsession—his real obsession with her. You can see the love he has for this girl. I said let's give him a camera and let him shoot his feelings for her."[93]

It wasn't the first time—nor would it be the last—that an exotic beach served as an advertising jewel case. But this time, the desert island was more than a set; it was an experience that anticipated the invention of reality television. The Calvin Klein brand had invited the two lovers to make strategic use of their love: one of them as model, the other as photographer. Mario Sorrenti understood precisely what the exercise was about. It had to be credible. Applying Corinne Day's method in an entirely different spirit, Sorrenti refused to collaborate with a crew of makeup artists, stylists, and lighting designers. Recalling the lack of makeup and lighting, Moss said years later, "Mario was like, 'You have to be naked, man—it's about purity; you have to be pure.'" Moss tried to resist but, "At the end of the day, you know, he had the control."[94]

The couple's relationship did not survive this exacting demand for "purity," but for the time being, the deserted island made it possible to isolate them from the outside world and guaranteed that the experiment would be carried out until the end. "Maybe this is just cinema vérité for the MTV generation," Calvin Klein's public-relations director Lynn Tesoro would say. Moss would recall: "I remember hearing Mario's voice in the other room going, 'I love you Kate, I love you Kate.' And I was like: 'What is that?' He was like: 'Well it's true man! It's true!' And I was like: 'You're mad.'"[95]

At that moment, and perhaps in spite of himself, Sorrenti was acting as a double agent: he was at once Kate's lover and the one directing their love. The intimacy between the photographer and his model, entirely different in nature from the intimacy governing their relationship, made the viewer complicit in its overexposure, as if the viewer were both witness and voyeur. This setup has since been widely used by reality television shows such as *Big Brother* and *Real World*, among others, which immerse real human beings in experiments that are both staged and improvised, half-acted and half-lived, and that force them to make strategic use of themselves under the gaze of others. The exoticism attached to the deserted island's distant shores was in this case reinforced by a sort of exoticism of intimacy, which transformed the Other into an object of curiosity as well as into a subject to be civilized.

This exercise represented the point where twenty-first-century reality met the "human zoos" of colonial expositions for which, from 1880 to 1930, European nations staged shows of "indigenous people" from their colonies. Their aim was to present the Other as a "savage," the object of a civilizing mission; now the goal tended to present the individuals as people to be coached and styled, the object of a valorization. Thus the stake in this operation may not have been to exhibit the intimate so much as to interiorize the model of a fashionable individual, the transformation of a social law into a psychic fact.

The Democratic Republic of Style

Mario Sorrenti's photographs were remarkable not for presenting Moss's alleged anorexia but for their simulation of the real. What one saw on billboards and television screens wasn't just an advertising image designed to lead consumers to buy Obsession, the perfume; the image was neither a real nor a fictional experience, but a simulated one that could be read as such. The dark shadows under Moss's eyes, her pale complexion, her look of anger or resignation, all are evidence of an experience that could be read entirely as advertising. Moss didn't use her beauty—a banal feature on the worldwide model market—to draw our attention; she used what was happening to her, a certain pathos that was particular to her actual experience. The Obsession campaign was an intrigue on a television set; a romance on a film stage, and in it, Moss was the object of her boyfriend's amorous and photographic fixation. The intrigue seemed limited to gazes.

In the campaign's most famous photograph—soon to be scribbled upon by those who protested that the image promoted anorexia—Moss posed on her stomach, naked on a black sofa, face turned toward the camera, her gaze somewhat exasperated. But exasperation hardly mattered as long as it contributed to making things look more real. "It's believable," Calvin Klein exclaimed when he saw Sorrenti's photos. "It's just like Mario feels about Kate. People want that reality."[96] From now on, what mattered for fashion and for marketing in general was not to simply sell clothes, but to associate them with possible attitudes and worlds that would sell them. To be sellable, products had to be the purveyors of narrative universes, the vehicles of universes. In a world given over to the shimmer of signs and the vertigo of suspicion, Kate Moss revealed herself as being capable of importing the signs of a credible realness to television screens, magazines, and city walls. "She is able to make things real," John Galliano, her Pygmalion, would say. Moss was like a meteor from a planet called experience, which conferred her added credibility as if by magic.

Within haute couture's immutable fixed universe, Corinne Day's photographs injected signs of life and blocks of the real, as well as a novelistic tension that fashion would adopt so as to align itself with the ideal types of mass culture. This new situation led magazine editors to favor making their editorial fashion pages into narratives, while top fashion designers transformed their runway shows into theater stages and the presentation of their collections into staged shows. The object of fashion was changing: it no longer included only garments but daily life as a whole. Style was no longer confined to clothes only, but extended to the way they were worn, the way they were "lived." This mutation was propitious ground for all kinds of misunderstandings, all kinds of misconceptions.

Indeed, the waif look modeled by Moss in the early 1990s carried a contradictory message. Within this style coexisted, on the one hand, the image of an abandoned child, of a neglected body left to its own devices—which meant the absence of care, and therefore, the opposite of cosmetics and fashion—and, on the other hand, the idea of a style, which implies the construction of an attitude and the mastery of appearances. The waif look, an anti-style, fused the ideas of abandonment and of mastery. The dream of a generation and the ideal of an era were meeting in the contradictory figure of Kate Moss. In magazines like *The Face* and *i-D*, where her work was regularly published, Day's photographs would have gone unnoticed. But in British *Vogue*, the photographs registered and legitimized fashion's tipping into mass culture. This tipping was what British fashion stylist Elliott Smedley stressed in an article about fashion photography in the 1990s: "Such images can work as a conventional marketing tool when used in a context where their audience will understand the dominant conventions, especially in fashion advertising, where they can promote a completely different lifestyle to that actually depicted. The prospective clients are not buying into a world of deprivation but into the usual ideal that anybody can be fashionable."[97]

In truth, the debates Day's photographs provoked did not oppose certain conceptions of morality or public-health concerns; they opposed two ages and two regimes of fashion: one of them, haute couture, was elitist; the other was democratic, belonged to mass culture, and had Kate Moss as ambassador. At once woman and child, girl and boy, Moss's androgynous body did not lend itself to an eroticization of childhood at all. Quite conversely, her body represented a desexualization of the female body, a neutering of gender. Transgender or post-gender, Moss was a symbol that could be mobilized at different levels and in all kinds of intrigues.

Therein lies the unbelievable misunderstanding about Moss's legendary leanness, which is in no way a symptom of anorexia. This leanness allowed her, in practical terms, to assume all kinds of intrigues and characters—one might call hers an avatar's leanness. All viewers—young or old, man or woman, from a ritzy neighborhood or the suburbs—could recognize themselves in her. Therefore, following this new declaration of "human and model rights," fashion now belonged to everyone. This revolution, which lasted throughout the year 1993, abolished the privileges of a world of fashion cut off from the social world, and lay the foundations for a new regime, the "democratic republic of style."

The Fashionable Individual Ideal

The "right to style" was the culmination of a long historical evolution of individualism, which can be documented in many ways. In his 1996 *Selbstversuch. Ein Gespräch mit Carlos Oliveira* ("Self-Intoxication: A Conversation with Carlos Oliveira"), German philosopher Peter Sloterdijk sketched this trend in a way that clearly illuminates the birth of this republic of style and its typical citizen, the fashionable individual.

According to Sloterdijk, eighteenth-century individualism corresponded to the novel form of which it was a contemporary—in which an individual grants himself a sort of "right of authorship to his own stories and opinions" and views his life as a novel. In the twentieth century, individuals began to claim the right not just to the novel of their lives but to their appearances as well. These are "all the people, high in color, whom you can now see hanging out downtown, with their Mohawks and paratrooper boots, behaving like synthetic-fur tiger lilies."[98]

But it takes more than style to define the typical late twentieth-century "designer individual." A fundamental

element is missing: the desire to conduct experiments on oneself. The bourgeois individual of the eighteenth century relied for the most part on the ancient scholastic concept of "self-preservation," which served as a kind of buttress limiting an individual's assertion of himself. This buttress had disappeared by the 1990s: self-assertion knew no limit; people had to be able to take self-experimentation "to the breaking point." The imperative of self-intensification had become inseparable from the experimentation principle, which bloomed and found legitimization in what was called "heroin chic." For Tom Ford, Gucci's creative director at the time, "The goal is to look like you've seen everything, done everything, been everywhere. It's an intimidating look, and the drug thing is the continuation of all that. If you look like you've been out all night, it conjures up all these images in your head."[99]

After 1993, the heroin chic look took over from the waif who, as noted, had become incompatible with the demands of the fashion industry, whose main goal remained to sell clothes and beauty products. Long associated with poor neighborhoods, despair, and AIDS, heroin now moved into good neighborhoods, where it acquired an aura of romanticism and gloominess. It permeated the air of the times all the way to the skin of models. According to Bill Mullen, then creative director of *Details* magazine, their skin was now clammy with "junkie sweats."[100]

Heroin chic expressed the desire to constantly have new experiences and to experiment with danger and limits in a society where the culture industries prized an incessant search for new sources of excitement. Everyone had to enhance his or her own worth. The idea of a sovereign self, master and owner of nature, thus found its paradoxical culmination in the sovereign individual who had no other relationship with himself than one of valorization, intensification, and styling.

Kate Moss was a veritable accelerator of experience, which explains why her influence persisted through the 1990s and into the twenty-first century. During the 1990s, she experienced no less than three successive mutations: from the grunge kid photographed by Corinne Day to John Galliano's Lolita "pursued by wolves," she finally acceded to the status of global brand, to becoming a vehicle for a narrative of permanent change. Neither psychology nor fortuitous encounters nor even the succession of happenstances of which legend is so fond can explain her success. Traveling from one continent to another and from

Victor Alfaro ready-to-wear, Spring/
Summer 1996.

one social universe to the next, this multi-business-card-
holding fashion salesperson was a mutating virus in an age
of sweeping mimetic epidemics, a worker bee who had a
knack for pollinating brands and styles. At the beginning
of the twenty-first century, Moss's status would undergo
another series of transformations, making her not only an
icon of Tony Blair's "Cool Britannia," but a contemporary art
muse and, according to some observers, a new myth.

4
A NEW MYTH?

ON MARCH 3, 2006, WHEN MOSS
appeared at the end of British designer Alexander McQueen's
runway show in the Louvre's Cour Carrée, she was greeted
with thunderous applause and expressions of surprise. The
Cour Carrée was the very same venue where, sixteen years
earlier, a fifteen-year-old Moss had first created a sensation
by literally running the length of the runway per Galliano's
direction, a plume on the battlefield of beauty, her crinoline
in the wind. This time around, she wasn't running; she was
spinning slowly in a movement that seemed shot in slow
motion, like a top about to topple, a tiny flame flickering
inside a glass pyramid, at once visible and elusive. Moss
was like a hologram or a specter who had come back to
taunt those who, a few months before, had decided her
media death. Her reappearance only reinforced what she
once had famously said, "The more they make me visible,
the more invisible I become." [101]

The Passion According to Kate Moss

Ever since the *Daily Mirror*'s September 15, 2005, front-page photograph, taken on the sly, showing Kate Moss with her nose in cocaine, the model had not been seen on the runways. Outrageously pixilated, as dirty as the tabloid paper on which it was printed, the picture had traveled around the world with two inseparable insulting words as its only passport: "Cocaine Kate."

Her agents had attempted to counter the scandal with flat excuses and stays in rehab. But the damage had been done. There were cancelled contracts, a flagging reputation. The downfall of the House of Moss was shaking up the entire profession. Some brands took this opportunity to distance themselves from her. Others defended the icon like central banks banding together to save a currency. The profession gathered rank. François-Henri Pinault—head of the PPR group, which owned both Gucci and Yves Saint Laurent—had these sensible words: "If we're using Kate Moss as a symbol of freedom, of transgression, we have to be honest. We can't use her image to convey these very messages and be surprised that she is transgressive in her private life."[102]

Dazed & Confused editor Jefferson Hack, the father of Moss's daughter, Lila Grace, born in 2002 (the couple had split up by the time of the scandal), gave a moving account of their former family life, which was entirely devoted to work. His description of his ex-girlfriend's mothering skills made her look worthy of a pietà. In the December 2005–January 2006 issue of French *Vogue*, John Galliano skewered the moral hypocrisy of Moss's accusers: "The fashion industry was right to stress Kate's immense influence on teenagers around the world," he explained to Sheryl Garratt, adding perfidiously that he rejoiced at the big clothing chains' concern for the health of the young and that he hoped they would extend this new concern to factories in developing countries, where a good amount of the items they sell were being made, and which, for a large part, relied on child labor.[103]

Kate Moss came out of her clinic for millionaires with the faith of a new convert: she spoke about addiction in Freudian tones and seemed eager to convince then-boyfriend Pete Doherty to follow her example. But the stubborn lover fled, unbelieving. The press reported on the ups and downs of Moss's breakup with the person deemed responsible for the scandal. Yet the couple continued to see each other in secret, much to their agents' and publicists' dismay.

Page 94: Alexander McQueen ready-to-wear, Fall/Winter 2006–7.
Above, left: Moss and Pete Doherty at the Glastonbury Music Festival, Somerset, England, 2005.
Above, right: Moss in New York City, September 2006.

During a previous stay in rehab in 1998, Moss had had her London house exorcized to rid it of evil spirits and memories. But now the smell of sulfur was attached to Moss herself. How was she to return to the center of attention other than as a fallen artist coerced into making amends? How was she to change her image while remaining herself? For a brand and an icon, the problem amounted to an existential dilemma. Going into crisis-communication mode would not be enough. A model can multiply "media coups," discover a sudden passion for impoverished children, invest insane amounts of money in the fight against cancer, and dress up entirely in heart-shaped red ribbons as an act of solidarity with AIDS victims—nevertheless, a model's purgatory is the runway. That is where the model had to be reborn.

In spring 2006, Alexander McQueen pulled off much more than an act of technological prowess: he orchestrated

a symbolic resurrection. Surrounded by models adorned
with wings and feathers, Moss reappeared like a ghost
bound in white bandages: she was Moss the angel at the
center of a full court of butterflies and birds.

A Symbolic Resurrection

Like other religions, fashion needs signs from the great
beyond when faith is flagging. Angel footsteps on deserted
runways are not enough. Neither are the see-through veils
fashion likes to drape around models. To not lose faith,
fashion needs miracles. And if needed, it calls technology
to the rescue. Fashion is often reproached with being
materialistic and superficial. This is a misconception. Fashion
is a mystique. It is the last religion. It needs believers, not
audiences, and even less, consumers.

Shopping has become more of a ritual than a mere act of
purchase. It is a celebration: one goes shopping as one would
go to a church service. Fashion erects intermittent temples,
cathedrals made of sequins and light. Proust understood
this well: he compared his oeuvre to a dress rather than to a

cathedral. Dresses are the cathedrals of fashion, and runway shows its processions. The two universes sometimes meet long enough for an eclipse or a snapshot, such as in the Sam Taylor-Wood photograph in which Moss stands in front of a church porch, a veil over her face, a tear in the corner of her eye, her gaze turned toward heaven as if she were a mystical Madonna. After the grunge years, the "monastic" style brought crosses and sackcloth dresses onto the runways. In 1994, in the highly sensitive context of the fatwa issued against Salman Rushdie, Karl Lagerfeld went so far as to print verses from the Koran on a dress worn by model Claudia Schiffer—until threats quickly made him take them off. Two years earlier, photographer Oliviero Toscani had illustrated fashion's permanent flirtation with religion by staging "The Kissing Nun" ad for Benetton, which presented a provocative kiss between a man of the cloth and a nun.

Fashion has its clergy, its pastors, its bishops. It also has its heretics and its sects. Despite the nickname "High Priestess of Fashion," Anna Wintour is its theologian, and American *Vogue*, which she's been running since 1988, is the bible of good taste. Every fall, Wintour's encyclopedic September issue decrees the season's trends, excommunicating heretics such as the poor waif, repudiated in 1993 in the name of sacrosanct glamour. Jean Paul Gaultier and Christian Lacroix derive their authority from the Catholic Church. There is some Calvinism in Lagerfeld. But the church has also had its Orthodox popes, people like Gianni Versace and Galliano. For his part, John Galliano believes in the resurrection.

The press spoke about a "hologram," but the Advertising Lab at M.I.T.—which is to the virtual world what the office of verification of miracles is to the sanctuary at Lourdes— straightened things out: the 3-D image of Kate Moss inside the pyramid was an application of the old "Pepper's ghost" principle. That principle was named after John Henry Pepper, a chemist who first engineered it on the occasion of an adaptation of the Charles Dickens novella titled *The Haunted Man* at London's Polytechnic Institute in 1862. Using panes of glass, specific lighting techniques, and a black room, Pepper succeeded in creating ghostlike images that could appear, disappear, and transform into one another, as today's morphing software allows us to do.

As engineered by Alexander McQueen and videographer Baillie Walsh for the designer's Paris ready-to-wear presentations, the performance was an updated version of Pepper's ghost. Four video screens projected a prerecorded image of

Moss onto the four sides of I.M. Pei's pyramid at the Louvre. As a result, the virtual image was visible from every angle, regardless of where one stood around the pyramid. The apparatus was extremely hard to set up, but it made the images appear in relief, an impression accentuated by the model's rotation as well as her white dress's undulating waves.

Never before had a model appeared to be so unreal, a shaky image in an alignment of light rays. Moss became an optical effect, a light phenomenon. She appeared and disappeared in a well of light, her face slightly flattened by the video projection. Angels are said not to have backs, only faces: here, McQueen had created a virtual angel, a pure phenomenon of belief. Moss could have been taken for a saint in levitation. Dancing in the night, her white ghost radiated the luminescence of transfigured bodies in biblical paintings.

Kate Moss's Mutations

Kate Moss's canonization did not take place in a day. It took two decades at the very least. Longevity is exceptional in the versatile world of fashion, which is subject to the dictates of seasons and only knows of one-day queens. "Modeling years are like dog years," James Sherwood wrote in the *Independent* in 1998. "For every year, think seven years of an average career. It is extraordinary, to say the least, that Kate has survived for ten years total with the unconditional love of her fans intact.... If she was a passive fashion Barbie doll, Kate wouldn't connect with us, but she is a whole package; the attitude, the look, and the energy of her time."[104]

"Since her debut, Kate has straddled three completely different fashion movements," Sherwood quoted photographer Nick Knight—the first to photograph Moss for American *Vogue*—as saying, "Moss was the gamine grunge princess of early nineties recession," Sherwood continued. "She was the face of CK1, the Calvin Klein scent that spelled optimism, inclusion, and innocence. Now heroin chic Kate and CK1 Kate have given way to sophisticated high-glam Kate." Moss's true talent lies here, in her ability to find herself in the right place at the right time, to electrify networks, to have presentments of and embody the evolutions the fashion world and mass culture go through—it lies in this more than it does in her languishing, lost-child airs or her alcohol and drug abuse.

With Labour's rise to power in 1997, Moss became the icon of Tony Blair's "Cool Britannia." Draped in the Union Jack, the new figurehead of the venerable house of Burberry embodied old England's mutation into a young, cool nation in the image of its new prime minister. This was the time when she crossed fashion's borders to become friendly with the artists, painters, musicians, and sculptors who would make her their muse. By entering into a relationship with Jefferson Hack, she married into the world of contemporary art and Young British Artists (YBAs), until she took on Pete Doherty and the pop rock scene. From a simple icon of consumerism, she became a muse of contemporary art, then transformed into a night angel nicknamed "Dracula," more transgressive than normative, more cyborg than goddess, a "trash" myth in the Internet age.

The Icon of "Cool Britannia"

As early as 1996, Tony Blair had expressed his desire to change Britain's image. Immediately after his election in 1997, the "Cool Britannia" campaign was launched, an operation designed to make over the image of the old monarchy and sell its new talents abroad. Under the guise of a marketing campaign, New Labour was undergoing a veritable ideological recasting: workers were no longer the agents of change, young people were. The party's new social base was the industry of culture, not traditional industry, a field that, according to Chris Smith, then-Secretary of State for Culture, Media, and Sport, included no more than a million people. In Labour's new stock of images, Andy Warhol's Factory had eclipsed Karl Marx's. The symbolic and semantic shift permeated New Labour's economic analysis as well as its political strategy.

Tony Blair's former advisor, economist Charles Leadbeater, has a particular predilection for movie metaphors. According to Leadbeater, corporate production is governed by the same rules as film production: many scripts are written, but only a few end up being made. He describes the phenomenon as the Hollywoodization of the labor market. Deep into the recession, Leadbeater invited young Brits to become "resilient" cultural entrepreneurs and consider the loss of a job as a script rejection, so as to quickly write another that would find a producer.

For New Labour, the "cultural industries" constituted what heavy industry was to Soviet five-year plans—at once the basis for future development and a powerful federating myth. At the heart of the new economic strategy of pump priming and job creation, cultural industries stood as the feather in the cap of Labour and the symbol of a rejuvenated and modernized Britain. "In de-industrialized regions the prospect of attracting some artists with the lure of cheap studio spaces [was] the most desirable outcome for policy makers," explained Angela McRobbie, a communications professor at London's Goldsmiths College. "It create[d] interesting stories for the press, it [held] the promise of gallery owners and more mainstream media companies moving in, and with these the whole panoply of coffee shops, bars and restaurants."[105] In fact, the hope for "regeneration" was not limited to urban zones; agricultural regions might also be reborn thanks to the Shoreditch effect, named after the London suburb that had been transformed into a bourgeois-bohemian enclave.

From one end of the country to the other, New Labour advisors were calling for "cultural regeneration," their language full of religious tones inspired by the speeches of Tony Blair, for whom "the model of culture and the arts as a source for moral and spiritual regeneration [was also a source] for creating better citizens."[106] This discourse became the new social utopia, a mythology that drew its heroes and gods from media personalities in fashion and show business, whose success proved that someone could make it even in times of crisis as long as he or she had talent. Associated with the rise of cultural industries, a new model for social success was inspired by J. K. Rowlings's "rags-to-riches" story, writing the first book in the Harry Potter series in an Edinburgh café. Such success stories allowed the wildest hopes to flourish and gave credence to the existence of a new cultural meritocracy that rewarded the talent and creativity of young artists from the working class.

Thus in Charles Leadbeater's eyes, designer Alexander McQueen represented the perfect example of the suburban youth with no training who became a haute couture star in a matter of years. It didn't matter that the new Givenchy director was not the outsider Tony Blair's advisor spoke about or that he had trained, like an entire generation of avant-garde designers, at Saint Martins. For Angela McRobbie, Leadbeater's mistake spoke to his desire to insist on the manner in which traditional barriers had been broken and had allowed new talents to be revealed. Success stories for fashion's enfants terribles were not so frequent, and in the end included just a few names: Stella McCartney, John Galliano, Alexander McQueen, and Vivienne Westwood. To these names, those of Damien Hirst, Marc Quinn, Sam

Taylor-Wood, Tracey Emin (born in Croydon, like Moss) were added, then exported as flag bearers for British creativity by the British Council. For Charles Leadbeater, they were evidence of a more open society, where "everyone had a chance to make it."

Throughout the first decade of the twenty-first century, Kate Moss occupied the center of the effervescence created and maintained by the ambiguous marriage of art, politics, and celebrity. The May 2007 issue of British *Vogue* asked seven young artists in the YBA group to turn Moss into a work of art. Among them were Tracey Emin, Jake and Dinos Chapman, and Sam Taylor-Wood. "You get the impression that she has been photographed by everyone, filmed by everyone, that she is forever in," said Taylor-Wood. "Yet every time she offers something different. She has this kind of constant vibration that gives off this unprecedented feeling."[107] Three months later, *W* magazine once again devoted forty editorial pages to Moss.

Photographers, painters, and sculptors were creating the twenty-first-century Kate Moss—she was no longer just a runway and magazine star, but a contemporary art muse. "Kate Moss is a cultural hallucination that we've all contributed to create," explained sculptor Marc Quinn. "She is the only person with this type of ubiquity and the muteness associated with the godlike figures created throughout history so we can project ourselves in them."[108]

In spring 2007, nine photographs of Kate Moss were on display at the National Portrait Gallery in London in an exhibition entitled *Face of Fashion*. At that time, Moss's portrait by Lucian Freud, sold at auction for nearly 6 million euros (almost 8 million U.S. dollars). A few years earlier, as the editor of the *History of Beauty*, Umberto Eco used a Herb Ritts photograph of Moss at the end of the book, along with three other contemporary photographs, to illustrate the book's conclusion: that it was now impossible to identify the aesthetic ideal.

What Is a Myth?

Can one truly speak of myth when speaking of Kate Moss? Isn't turning what may be only a simple media phenomenon into a timeless myth going a bit too far? Does Moss have a place next to Greta Garbo, Audrey Hepburn, and Marilyn Monroe, all of whom Hollywood made into universal and eternal figures? Some will cry blasphemy. But what is a

myth? Has talent or genius ever been sufficient to explain the existence of a myth? And is there anything in common between Garbo and Hathor, the Egyptian goddess of love; between Hepburn and the Greeks' Aphrodite; or between Monroe and the Romans' Venus?

If one were to find antecedents for Kate Moss in mythology, one would have to look to Daphne, who, with the help of her father, Peneus, was transformed into a laurel tree to escape the avid pursuit of Apollo. The myth of Daphne and Apollo has inspired a great many painters and sculptors, among them Italian sculptor Gian Lorenzo Bernini. Now in Rome's Borghese Gallery, Bernini's marble sculpture (1622–25) represents a fashion designer's dream come true: capturing the interplay of gaze and desire, the work embodies the hunter, the prey, and the chase in a single movement. It shows the flutter in Apollo's garment and the wind blowing in the nymph's loose hair as Daphne's half-opened mouth continues to cry for help even as the bark tightens around her body.

For Plato, mythmaking consisted in fashioning models of identification, "fictions" in the etymological sense of *fingere*, "to model" or "to shape." Plato even spoke about mythmaking as a "plastic" art. For him a myth was an acting fiction—today we would call it performative—whose role was to propose, if not impose, models of identification or an ideal individual to social groups or even an entire people. This process was both symbolic and social; it consisted of manufacturing an acting dream that was an object of belief and functioned like a religion. Thus, there is more than a simple analogy between the origin myths that fashioned humankind's behaviors and contemporary myths crafted by the fashion and media industries.

Roland Barthes distinguished between two mythical moments in the twentieth century, corresponding to the two ages of film: silent and talkies, Greta Garbo and Audrey Hepburn. Barthes's analysis is valuable in that it brings into relief the suprapersonal character of myth; his modern myths are not the result of a culture of merit or a hierarchy of beauty. What allows Barthes to establish a distinction between them is neither their mysterious powers nor exceptional qualities, nor even the trials one has experienced; it is technique. In silent movies, silence was associated with a specific kind of impassible beauty. The movies lent themselves to the contemplation of the face, which talkies would come to disturb. "The face of Garbo is an idea," Barthes wrote, "that of Hepburn, an event."[109]

Garbo's face "has the snowy thickness of a mask," Barthes wrote, adding that it was "not drawn but sculpted in something smooth and friable, at once perfect and ephemeral." It was a totemic face that brings to mind Marilyn's ageless whiteness, on which she "worked" with her makeup artist several hours a day so it would "reappear," as indelible as a logo, with its red lips, black mole, and peroxide blondness. This anachronistic Marilyn belongs to the mythical age of silent movies more than it does in that of talkies. This hypothesis would confirm what her biographers have said was the pain Monroe felt when speaking her lines, as well as her preference for being photographed rather than filmed. Indeed, with the advent of talkies, the face was no longer able to exert its fatal attraction; instead it was the slim, elongated silhouette and the proud bearing that harmonizes distinction and modernity, aristocracy and efficacy that did. For Barthes, Audrey Hepburn's "peculiar thematics (woman as child, woman as kitten)" embodied this mutation. The myth came down from heaven to settle at the heart of consumer society. The model-actress was distinguished by a modernist look, a new feminine ideal that was avant-gardist, with short hair, an androgynous body, and a swan neck, which showed to advantage everything she wore.

This transformation was not exactly without precedent. It had manifested itself right after World War II with the first pictures of female athletes. Women were represented in movement, not simply in glamour poses. This realistic representation offered modern women an image with which they were able to identify. Yet it was indeed in the movies that the metamorphosis was the most remarkable. "Garbo still belongs to that moment in cinema when capturing the human face still plunged audiences in the deepest ecstasy," Barthes wrote, "when one literally lost oneself in a human image as one would in a philtre, where the face represented a kind of absolute state of the flesh, which could be neither reached nor renounced. A few years earlier the face of Valentino was causing suicides; that of Garbo still partakes of the same rule of Courtly Love, where the flesh gives rise to mystical feelings of perdition." For his part, filmmaker Federico Fellini is believed to have once said, "Garbo was the founder of a religious order called cinema."

A Venus Bound for Our Times

Following the "terror" that the "divine" Garbo inspired came the "charm" emanating from Audrey Hepburn's svelte silhouette and aristocratic bearing. Greta's beauty gave rise to a cult—in which she officiated—whereas Audrey's charm merely worked. In the transition between the two mythic figures, a certain desacralization of female beauty—a form of secularization of the myth—was thus made manifest. Kate Moss embodies a third mythological age, that of the protean woman: what played a role in the construction of her media legend was no longer a face that was unchangeable in its perfection, nor an experience whose singularity was unchangeable: it was her ability to transform herself. At the turn of the twenty-first century, Moss modeled a new subject that was adaptable to any circumstance and was able to constantly reinvent herself. With her, substance became plastic; she acquired new characteristics: malleability and even volatility.

Kate Moss radicalized the fall from essence to substance observed between Garbo and Hepburn. She became a fungible substance, unstable and mutating matter. As previously noted, for Calvin Klein, Moss embodied the Obsession perfume and, like it, had the power to evaporate. In 2000, Marc Quinn made a life-size ice sculpture of Moss that was designed to melt over a period of a few months. The work was exhibited in a refrigerator specifically engineered to allow it to dissolve a little every day, a metaphor for the ephemeral character of any activity or construction. "It's the perfect metaphor for the way in which we consume her beauty," Quinn told journalist Sheryl Garratt in late 2005, when she was visiting his studio to report her December 2005–January 2006 French *Vogue* article. "As the ice melts, Kate evaporates in the gallery and people are able to literally inhale her," Quinn explained. According to the sculptor, the experience was "eucharistic."

During her visit, Garratt discovered small framed objects containing stains of organic matter held in suspension between sheets of glass. Like the scientists working on the "human genome" project, who collected and colored cells in order to map out the genotype, Quinn created human portraits from cells collected inside his subjects' cheeks. "Kate's hasn't been shown in public yet," Quinn said, adding: "As it is made with her DNA, it is at once the most faithful portrait of the model ever made, and the only one in which she is not immediately recognizable."

In 2006, Quinn chose to represent Moss as a contortionist, arms and legs intertwined, which, according to the artist, expressed the distorted images that both the media and our unconscious desires had imposed on her emblematic figure. Titled *Sphinx*, the solid-gold sculpture was the largest statue made since pharaonic Egypt. Exhibited at the British Museum, the statue represents the model as agile, flexible, and malleable to the point of transformism, embodying the dominant values of the new culture of capitalism. "It's the portrait of an image that has been distorted by our collective desire," Quinn explained. "It's a mirror image of ourselves, a Venus bound for our times." After the "Cocaine Kate" scandal, the sculptor would give his works new meaning, telling Garratt: "What's interesting now is that for me, they are like crucifixions. After all they've done to her, suddenly these contorted poses appear all the more pertinent."

A Neoliberal Destiny

Throughout the preceding chapters, using Kate Moss as a prism, we have observed, by approximation, the emergence of a new subject—one that is liquid, flexible, adaptable, who makes strategic uses of herself and pushes self-experimentation to the breaking point: this is the very definition of the neoliberal subject. In his 1979 lectures at the Collège de France, Michel Foucault stressed that neoliberalism did not apprehend individuals as consumers but rather as producers, and that it sought to "replace a *homo oeconomicus* who is a partner in exchange with a *homo oeconomicus* who is his own entrepreneur."[110]

It was no longer sufficient then, as it was during the postwar boom, to impose a mode of consumption consisting of a kit of accessories manufactured for the most part by the food, home-appliance, and automobile industries to satisfy humankind's need for objects. In a world saturated with objects, it was the subject him- or herself that had to become value or (human) capital, by building a "portfolio of conducts" and proving an ability to change according to the circumstances. Extending Foucault's analysis, the philosopher Michel Feher speaks of a neoliberal condition, which defines each of us as a stock of skills, both innate and conquered, actual and potential, or better yet, as a stock of skills eager to appreciate or, put another way, to ward off our depreciation. This portfolio of possible behaviors is meaningless if individuals are unable to mobilize and change them. "All one knows of human capital is the following," Feher writes: "(1) the subjects that it defines seek to appreciate and value themselves,

such that their life may be thought of as a strategy aimed at self-appreciation; (2) all of their behaviors and all the events affecting them (in any existential register) are liable to cause the subjects either to appreciate or to depreciate themselves; and (3) it is therefore possible to govern subjects seeking to increase the value of their human capital, or more precisely, to act on the way they govern themselves, by inciting them to adopt conducts deemed valorizing and to follow models for self-valuation that modify their priorities and inflect their strategic choices."[111]

But how is one to mobilize all those possible behaviors? Being competent isn't sufficient anymore; or rather, the nature of the necessary skills has changed: what is needed now is a narrative skill. The appreciation of the subject, a process during which he acquires an exchange value on the social market, now requires placing the individual inside a narrative that must render credible in the eyes of others the person's ability to exchange and change, an ability to transgress codes while remaining a player within mass culture and its media sphere. The liberal tradition's *homo oeconomicus* is no more, he who was able to optimize his interests, a great calculator before the eternal. It is now time for *homo ludens*, himself increasingly becoming *homo narrens*, his own narrator, prepared to do anything to draw the attention of his peers, who are themselves in a similar disposition. This gives life in society the character, rhythm, and costumes of a runway show (or carnival), in which one is at once the designer, the director, and the narrator of oneself, in a performance that is life itself. In this desperate quest for the "novelistic," of which reality television is both a symptom and a laboratory, the subject is condemned to the intensive valorization of his presentation and narrative resources, given that the transmissibility of experiences (and the exchangism of humankind) requires the "narrativization" of individuals.

"[T]he most important developments of modern life," observes James B. Twitchell, the author of *Branded Nation*,[112] lie in "the endless tying of fictions to the fabricated stuff of everyday life." As a result, the ideal of the "self-made man" takes on the features of a storyteller whose narrative extols competitive values (fighting, being strong, succeeding), and more important, who is able to give himself a "novelistic" aura and mutate to become an intense subject that adopts "memorable behaviors" that are "worth being told." This pleonastic redoubling

Opposite: To launch her collection for Topshop in 2007, Moss posed in a dress of her design in the window of the retailer's flagship store in London.

111

locks the subject inside a neoliberal form of quixotism, in which the subject must accomplish the ritual act of a social performance that is itself ritualized in the extreme, all at the expense of a foreclosure of meaning and experience. As Joseph Conrad wrote of his protagonist in *Lord Jim*: "Romance had singled Jim for his own— and that was the true part of the story, which otherwise was all wrong."[113]

In fact, ever since Cervantes, the novel has been both the privileged observatory and the laboratory of the self-realizing behaviors that define today's neoliberal subject. Indeed, what is a character in a novel other than a "portfolio of behaviors"—to use Michel Feher's expression—from which he draws depending on the situations with which he is faced, and which he attempts to use strategically? In adopting the "style" of the heroic knights, Don Quixote is willing himself to be "heroic" and "legendary." He mimes supposedly heroic behaviors in the hopes of acquiring an "aura" that exists solely in books. Emma Bovary is the ancestor of today's tabloid heroines: she adopts magical behaviors (taking lovers) that might ultimately confer to her the "novelistic" character (glamour) her life lacks. In Emma's "somewhat perverse nature," Flaubert revealed a woman full of "fake poetry" and "fake feeling," a form of individuation that was new at the time but has become common in today's Second Life era, which leads to the petrifying of human experience into novelistic clichés and ready-made stories. This "neo-Bovarism" lies at the heart of individual "celebrity-making strategies," which are part and parcel of neoliberalism's own management of desires and bodies.

The docile individual of disciplinary societies gives way to the strategist individual, who is now capable of both adopting and changing behaviors and is subject to an imminent law of self-valorization and self-intensification instead of a transcendent authority. From a disciplinary society that practiced the taming of bodies, we have gone on to a "fashion" society in which everyone must "perform" his or her life at every instant and adopt behaviors that might accrue or lose value, like stocks in an exchange. This situation implies a form of self-control that is no less demanding than was expected in the disciplinary society: it is about making strategic use of oneself in a society where the supreme value is no longer located outside the individual but rather woven from the person's actions and tactics.

In her series of plays titled *Prinzessinnendramen: Der Tod und das Mädchen I–III und IV–V* ("Princess Plays: Death and the Maiden I–III and IV–V"), from 2002, Austrian writer Elfriede Jelinek, the 2004 Nobel Prize winner in Literature, had Jackie Kennedy utter the following words: "In order to captivate others, you have to be captivated by yourself." Such is the neoliberal condition: "Make lovely movements with your head, and then tie up all the movements inside one photograph, tie them down like as many hostages of yourself. As many lovers of yourself.... You have to remain quiet, but in the noisiest manner possible within the silence, to inspire sensations in others, just like you get a sick person to take his medicine."[114] In this context, fashion becomes a laboratory for a new human condition defined by a subject bound to incessant and intensive experimentation on herself. Insofar as she is constantly inventing herself within a redistribution of hybrid signs of identity and a dizzying ballet of life forms and habitus, Kate Moss is this subject's prototype.

To reach the status of digital icon, Moss has lost all substance. She is shining in the transparency of the immaterial. She doesn't incarnate anything; she is modeling the new relationships to the body, gender, and the species instituted by neuroscience, biotechnology, and the digital revolution. She is also disseminating an era's ideal types, which outline the behavior of a new subject. Gone are the models to be imitated; gone are Hollywood's goddesses. Ours is not a time for figureheads but for mutants. As a cyborg-woman, Kate Moss is making the status of the model mutate from imitation to simulation. Her lean body, as skinny as a letter or a code, has nothing to do with anatomy anymore. Rather, it has to do with the lexicon of branding and the technique of morphing. Moss is modeling a life-program that is the quintessential neoliberal destiny.

What is to be learned from this "Mossian" destiny? That we must become seasoned strategist subjects capable of making intensive use of our skills and affects so that we present the best possible image of ourselves. That there is no other relationship to the self than this ceaseless valorization assisted by all kinds of personal development experts. That the choices individuals now make are limited either to a life that is exchangeable, therefore designed, redesigned, and coached, or to a nondesigned life that is not worth anything. In this exclusionary logic, we are all British models.

CONCLUSION
GODDESS OR CYBORG?

—————————————————————————
—————————————————————————
—————————————————————————
—————————————————————————
—————————————————————————
—————————————————————————

THE IMAGE IS ALL OVER THE INTERNET.
This one was not created by a famous photographer but
by a digital handyman. It shows Kate Moss taking off her
sweater, revealing a mechanical structure articulated with
suspension springs instead of her lower abdomen and hips.
Until now, there was a visible Kate, a flood of images on
fashion magazines covers; and a readable Kate, a stock of
anecdotes repeated ad nauseum in the tabloids, women's
magazines, and biographies. There was Kate's body, shot
from every angle, and the corpus of her written lives. In this
image knocked together on the Internet, the visible body is
fused with the written body. The technique of morphing has
created a written and coded cyborg-body.

For the Greeks, the presence of a writing tablet in a dream represented a woman, because "women bear the impression of all kinds of letters." For his part, Thomas Mann considered a life in myth as "a life in quotations." Kate Moss's legend conforms to these two definitions. She is a "written" woman who bears the impression of all kinds of letters; a "life in quotations," measured in terms of "occurrences" on the Internet: there were some 14 million in the fall of 2009, a much higher number than those of her modeling peers Cindy Crawford and Naomi Campbell, and that of actor Clint Eastwood, but close to the peaks of occurrences recorded for a mythical figure like Marilyn Monroe.

Google is the greatest mythographer of our time. In its pixel- and algorithm-dense firmament, new digital myths are being written. Google establishes the hierarchy of deities on the Web and draws their navigation maps. Kate Moss is one of Google's unquestioned goddesses, a Calypso with

Page 114: Moss in an advertising campaign for Roberto Cavalli's Spring/Summer 2006 collection. **Above:** Moss and Jamie Hince arrive at the Ritz Hotel in Paris, January 2011. Moss married Hince in July 2011.

mysterious powers to captivate, or a modern Daphne who is able to metamorphose so as to escape her media hounds. She might also be borrowing from Perseus, with a Longchamp or Gucci bag in which to put Medusa's head; with Hades's helmet, which makes one invisible even to the paparazzi, and a pair of winged sandals (Saint-Tropez style) to flee when needed. Her ubiquity can be measure by her speed of liberation (an aeronautics term), and her trips play an important role in the construction of her legend, which stresses the endurance of a woman who changes time zones several times a week, defying jet lag.

A new feminine ideal, mobile and mutant, at once in pursuit and in flight, is replacing the definitions of beauty as substance and identity (à la Greta Garbo and Marilyn Monroe) and beauty as "anthropological" standard (à la Claudia Schiffer). If the Marilyn myth as revisited by Andy Warhol relied on the infinite duplication of the same face suddenly heavy with quasi-divine ubiquity, the Kate Moss myth defies time through metamorphosis. The former ensured her omnipresence through the identical repetition of the same logo-face; the other builds her empire on transformation. Warhol had created a myth for the age of the copy machine—no Marilyn without Xerox. For its part, the Kate Moss myth is a contemporary of Second Life avatars, cloning, and morphing software.

The image of a cyborg Kate Moss, both organism and machine, is part of a series of photomontages titled "Celebrity Cyborgs" published in 2004 on fx.worth 1000.com, a site for retouched-photo fans, which shows such celebrities as Alicia Keys, Madonna, Tom Cruise, Gisele Bündchen, and Heidi Klum, all transformed into hybrid creatures, half-human and half-machine, organic and nonorganic. Looking through these morphing software–altered photographs, one discovers a cyborg's stock of images that combines bodily elements and materials and always functions along the same pairings: eyes/camera, nerves/threads, brain/clock. A disjointed half-face shows a hybrid skeletal structure, half-bone, half-metal. A missing cheek reveals a maze of electrical wiring and metallic elements. Instead of hands, we see articulated prosthetics; suction cups prick spines as in *The Matrix*. Unzipped below the chest, a body is made of an interesting mess reminiscent of an old television set. The robot shows under the skin, and the skull turns out to be an optical machine, a watch-making mechanism, or a maze of electronic components.

The cyborg's stock of images expresses the ideal of limitless individual mutability beyond distinctions of gender, character, and species. In the latter part of the twenty-first century's first decade, this ideal took hold of fashion and inspired haute couture collections from Alexander McQueen, Rei Kawakubo, and Gareth Pugh. Fashion cannot be content with dressing its models anymore. It makes them mutate into women with android looks, women-giraffes and, for Alexander McQueen, cyborg-women with hair in a sheath held up high at the back, like the antlers of young deer with hooves of moss.

The fashion woman is now a chrysalis in the image of the Rei Kawakubo models trapped inside a transparent, cocoonlike fabric, a silky envelope masking their metamorphosing faces. Fashion is reinventing the feminine somewhere between cyborg robots and classical beauties. In its workshops, fashion is experimenting with new relationships to the body, gender, and race. "United Colors of Benetton" deals with the color of skin as a painter's palette. Echoing her colleague Sarah Franklin, the author of several books about cloning, embryos, and stem cells, Donna Haraway, a professor and chair of the History of Consciousness Program at the University of California Santa Cruz, boldly asserts: "Race becomes a fashion accessory." [115]

Fashion cultivates the ideal of "pan-humanity," a synthesis made of combinations of elements of garment and identity that owes as much to bytes as it does to clothes. The status of modeling is changing: from one of imitation, it has become one of stimulation, belonging in the lexicon of branding and the technique of morphing. Fashion has become an operational mode.

On the cover of its September 1994 issue, *Mirabella* magazine featured a computer-generated woman's face created from many photographs of women from every ethnic background. With this cover, *Mirabella* was following in the footsteps of *Time* magazine, which had published a special issue about immigration titled "The New Face of America" one year earlier. The issue was illustrated by the "morphed portrait" of a female created by the computer-generated crossing of several races, set against a background showing a matrix of her cybergenetic kin. The image was put together with the first morphing software available for personal computers, Morph 2.0, a product of Gryphon Software Corporation. Morphing software has been put to much use since, by

Moss at Uniqlo's Spring/Summer
2010 presentation during London
Fashion Week, September 2009.

scientific researchers and university professors as much as
by special-effects artists for movies and law enforcement
for criminal sketches.

The individual who brought the ideal of morphing
to its highest degree of perfection and absurdity was
Michael Jackson. The singer used all the available bodily
technologies—from costumes to plastic surgery to video
clips to computer-generated transformations—to remodel
himself, modifying his age, gender, and "race" markers in the
process. Michael Jackson was the emblem of the identity
hybridization now presented as the ideal of the new global
world. Quoting another feminist author, Ramona Fernandez,
Haraway states, "His transmuting body enacts and re-enacts
the multiple problematics of race, generation, and gender,"
adding that Jackson metamorphosed into a creature that was
"neither white nor black, male nor female, man nor woman,
old nor young, human nor animal, historical person nor
mythological figure, homosexual nor heterosexual."[116]

"I would rather be a cyborg than a goddess,"[117] Haraway provocatively declared in 1991. In doing so, she was dismissing the types of feminism and humanism solidly supported by the ancient dualisms of female/male, nature/culture, creature/artifact. And instead of rejecting the mutations that were taking place as "unnatural" or "anti-humanist," Haraway opened up a new critical space, inviting feminists to create new narratives as an alternative to patriarchal origin stories. Haraway was bringing up the problem of power, which constituted the most interesting aspect of her approach and was not couched in terms of influence or ideological conditioning but rather of writing, coding, and narrative.

From time immemorial, patriarchal power—be it familial, entrepreneurial, or colonial—has been legitimized and perpetuated through narratives and origin myths. The novel fact that is radically transforming the struggle for emancipation today is that narrative power now lies at the heart of textual technologies—the technologies that write the world, biotechnology and microelectronics. "Pygmalion himself has been morphed; he has become a computer program," Haraway wrote, adding "These figures of the new humanity look like I imagine a catalog of replicants for sale off-world in *Blade Runner* might look—young, beautiful, talented, diverse, and programmed to fulfill the buyer's wishes and then self-destruct. Unlike the terrible white-supremacist scenes of *Birth of a Nation* in 1915, nothing about race and ethnicity in *Time*'s 'Rebirthing of a Nation' speaks about racial domination, guilt, and hatred.... Its violence consists in the evacuation of histories of domination and resistance ... *through* technological ... reproduction.... In this liberal, antiracist, and technophilic exercise ... [all] the bloody history caught by the ugly word *miscegenation* is missing in the sanitized term *morphing*.... It is the resolute absence of history, of the fleshy body that bleeds, that scares me."[118]

Presented as an ironic and poetic myth, Haraway's *A Manifesto for Cyborgs: Science, Technology and Socialist Feminism in the 1980s*, published in 1991, opened the way for a politics of counternarratives. "Cyborg politics is the struggle for language," Haraway wrote, "and the struggle against perfect communication, against the one code that translates all meaning perfectly.... [Its] tools are often stories, retold stories, versions that reverse and displace the hierarchical dualisms of organized identities…. In retelling origin stories, cyborg authors subvert the central myths of origin of Western culture."[119]

At the end of this journey into mass subculture as illuminated by Kate Moss's prismatic figure, the following alternative comes to mind: has the fashionable society already triumphed, and are we condemned to the state of models? Or has the neoliberal model been so shaken by the crisis of 2007–8 that a crisis arose in the "cosmetics-industrial" complex, whose genesis and consolidation have been broadly sketched here? In this case, Moss would simply be the icon and symptom of a now-obsolete neoliberal system, and her power over our minds would now be reaching its end. Nothing is less certain. The conservative revolution and its neoliberal politics have indeed made cunning use of the sociotechnical changes derived from neuroscience, biotechnology, and the digital revolution, and these changes remain inexorable, upsetting the conditions and the forms of subjection. Hence there is no reason to expect that the neoliberalist crisis will result in the spontaneous disappearance of the models of identification and myths it has generated. The technological revolution framing and formatting mass culture is, without a doubt, the most powerful that humanity has ever known because of the universal character of its consciousness-penetration techniques.

Narratives of power are no longer written only in books and on screen but instead at the heart of the new technologies that code bodies and guide behaviors through powerful federating myths. Fashion has become a performative field in which narratives and counternarratives, fictions of power and counternarrations, face off. The thread of these narratives is woven in a politics of reproduction. Therein lies the decisive challenge from which depends the very idea of the individual, of his origins, of his gender, of his relationships with other species, of his freedom, and of his story. His challenge is about language and the possible against the political management of bodies and desires. In the enigmatic figure of the cyborg, the dream of anthropogenesis, the myth of human self-generation lives on. As early as 1934, Polish writer Bruno Schulz had foreseen its imminence in "Tailors' Dummies," one of the short stories in his collection titled *The Street of Crocodiles*: "We want to create man a second time, in the shape and semblance of a tailor's dummy."[120]

Chapter Endnotes

INTRODUCTION

1. *The Guardian*, May 27, 2006.

2. As quoted by Françoise-Marie Santucci, *Kate Moss: Première biographie d'une icône*, Flammarion, Paris, 2008, p. 64.

3. Ibid., p. 64.

4. As quoted by Sheryl Garratt, "Million Dollar Baby," French *Vogue*, December 2005–January 2006, p. 209.

5. Katherine Kendall, *Kate Moss: Model of Imperfection*, Chamberlain Bros., New York, 2005, p. 2.

6. Marie Desplechin, "La Vie Rêvée de Kate Moss" [Kate Moss's Dream Life], *L'Express*, December 1, 2006.

7. Ernst Kris and Otto Kurz, *Legend, Myth, and Magic in the Image of the Artist*, Yale University Press, New Haven, CT, 1981.

8. Angela Buttolph, *Kate Moss Style: Inside the World's Most Famous Wardrobe*, Century, London, 2008, p. 6.

9. Françoise-Marie Santucci, *Kate Moss: Première biographie*, p. 63.

10. Pierre Bourdieu, "L'Illusion Biographique" [The Biographical Illusion], *Actes de la Recherche en Sciences Sociales*, no. 62–63, pp. 69–72.

11. As quoted by Françoise-Marie Santucci, *Kate Moss: Première biographie*, p. 118.

12. Bret Easton Ellis, *Glamorama*, Alfred A. Knopf, New York, 1999, p. 527.

CHAPTER 1

13. Françoise-Marie Santucci, *Kate Moss: Première biographie*, p. 50.

14. Ibid., p. 50.

15. Ibid., p. 62.

16. Ibid., p. 61.

17. Ibid., p. 51.

18. Ibid., p. 52.

19. As quoted by Angela Buttolph, *Kate Moss Style*, p. 21.

20. As quoted by Françoise-Marie Santucci, *Kate Moss*, p. 58.

21. Walter Benjamin, "The Work of Art in the Age of Its Technological Reproductibility," *Selected Writings*, edited by Howard Eiland and Michael W. Jennings, Belknap Press of Harvard University Press, Cambridge, MA, 2003.

22. As quoted by Katherine Kendall, Kate *Moss: Model of Imperfection*, pp. 16–17.

23. Douglas Coupland, *Generation X: Tales for an Accelerated Culture*, St. Martin's Press, New York, 1991.

24. As quoted by Katherine Kendall, *Kate Moss*, p. 17.

25. Jean Baudrillard, "La guerre du Golfe n'aura pas lieu" [The Gulf War will not take place], *Libération*, January 4, 1991.

26. Jean-François Lyotard, *The Postmodern Condition: A Report on Knowledge*, Manchester University Press, 1984.

27. Christian Salmon, *Storytelling: La machine à fabriquer des histoires et à formater les esprits*, La Découverte, Paris, 2007.

28. Christian Salmon, *Verbicide. Du bon usage des cerveaux humains disponibles*, Climats, Castelnau-Le-Rez, 2005 (reissued by Actes Sud, coll. "Babel," Arles, 2007).

29. Walter Benjamin, "The Storyteller," p. 8.

30. Douglas Coupland, *Generation X*, p. 8.

31. Paul Ricoeur, *Time and Narrative* (*Temps et Récit*), 3 vols., translated by Kathleen McLaughlin and David Pellauer, University of Chicago Press, 1984, 1985, 1988.

32. Douglas Coupland, *Generation X*, pp. 23–24.

33. Ibid., pp. 13–14.

34. Don DeLillo, *Falling Man*, Scribner, New York, 2007, p. 29.

35. Douglas Coupland, *Generation X*, p. 14.

36. Ibid., p. 39.

37. Sheryl Garratt, "Million Dollar Baby," French *Vogue*, December 2005–January 2006, p. 211.

38. As quoted by Paul Jobling, *Fashion Spreads: Words and Image in Fashion Photography Since 1980*, Berg, Oxford, 1999, p. 40.

39. As quoted by Angela Buttolph, *Kate Moss Style*, p. 22.

40. Iwona Blazwick, "Feel No Pain," *Art Monthly*, November 1998, p. 7.

41. Rebecca Arnold, *Fashion, Desire and Anxiety*, Rutgers University Press, New Brunswick, NJ, 2001, p. 59.

42. As quoted by Rebecca Arnold, *Fashion, Desire and Anxiety*, p. 82.

43. Jean Baudrillard, *Symbolic Exchange and Death*, Sage Publications, London, 1993, p. 94.

44. Walter Benjamin, "The Work of Art in the Age of Its Technological Reproductibility."

CHAPTER 2

45. As quoted by Angela Buttolph, *Kate Moss Style*, p. 22.

46. Ibid., p. 53.

47. As quoted by Sheryl Garratt, "Million Dollar Baby," French *Vogue*, December 2005–January 2006, p. 213.

48. Françoise-Marie Santucci, *Kate Moss: Première biographie*, p. 64.

49. As quoted by Naomi Klein, *No Logo. Taking Aim at the Brand Bullies*, Picador, New York, 1999, p. 111.

50. Ibid., p. 75.

51. As quoted by Sheryl Garratt, "Million Dollar Baby," p. 209.

52. *The Independent*, May 2003.

53. As quoted by Françoise-Marie Santucci, *Kate Moss: Première biographie*, p. 66.

54. As quoted by Katherine Kendall, *Kate Moss: Model of Imperfection*, p. 21.

55. As quoted by Angela Buttolph, *Kate Moss Style*, p. 4.

56. Naomi Klein, *No Logo*, p. 75.

57. As quoted by Françoise-Marie Santucci, *Kate Moss: Première biographie*, p. 65.

58. As quoted by Angela Buttolph, *Kate Moss Style*, p. 42.

59. Françoise-Marie Santucci, *Kate Moss: Première biographie*, p. 116.

60. As quoted by Angela Buttolph, *Kate Moss Style*, p. 197.

61. Ibid., p. 53.

62. Ingrid Sischy, "The Kate Moss Story," *Interview*, March 1999.

63. As quoted by Angela Buttolph, *Kate Moss Style*, p. 196.

64. Roland Barthes, *The Fashion System*, Jonathan Cape, London, 1983, pp. 260–61.

65. Patrícia Soley-Beltran, "Modelling Femininity," in "Spectacular Women," *European Journal of Women's Studies*, November 3, 2004, p. 9.

66. Richard Sennett, *The Culture of the New Capitalism*, Yale University Press, New Haven, CT, 2006, p. 40.

67. Ibid., pp. 3–5.

68. *Sunday Times* (London), May 7, 1988.

69. Richard Sennett, *The Culture of the New Capitalism*, pp. 3–5.

70. Zygmunt Bauman, *Liquid Modernity*, Polity Press, Cambridge (UK), 2000.

71. As quoted by Sheryl Garratt, "Million Dollar Baby," p. 209.

CHAPTER 3

72. Roland Barthes, *The Fashion System*, p. 261.

73. Ibid., p. 261.

74. Gilles Lipovetsky, *La Troisième Femme. Permanence et révolution du féminin* [The Third Woman: Permanence and revolution of the feminine], Gallimard, Paris, 1997, pp. 216–217.

75. As quoted by Mark Harvey, "Drug Chic Gets a Shock," *Daily Mail*, May 23, 1997.

76. Amy Spindler, "The 90s Version of the Decadent Look," *New York Times*, May 7, 1996.

77. Michel Foucault, *Discipline and Punish: The Birth of the Prison*, Vintage Books, New York, 1995.

78. Roland Barthes, *The Fashion System*, p. 261.

79. Roland Barthes, ibid., p. 262.

80. Christian Salmon, *Storytelling*.

81. As quoted by Fred Vermorel, *Addicted to Love: Kate Moss*, Omnibus Press, London, 2006, p. 60.

82. *Orlando Sentinel*, February 5, 1994.

83. As quoted by Fred Vermorel, *Addicted to Love*, p. 58.

84. As quoted by Cécile Dumas, "Le corps du délit" ("The body and its crimes"), *Libération*, September 29, 2006.

85. Amy M. Spindler, "How Fashion Killed the Unloved Waif," *New York Times*, September 27, 1994.

86. Ibid.

87. Ibid.

88. Ibid.

89. Hilton Als, "Buying Fantasy," *The New Yorker*, June 10, 1996.

90. Pierre Bourdieu, *Sociology in Question*, Sage Publications, London, 1994.

91. Marthe Robert, *Origins of the Novel*, translated by Sacha Rabinovitch, Indiana University Press, Bloomington, IN, 1980.

92. Clarissa Pinkola Estés, *Women Who Run with the Wolves*, Houghton Mifflin, New York, 1992.

93. As quoted by Amy M. Spindler, "Patterns," *New York Times*, June 8, 1993.

94. As quoted by Fred Vermorel, *Addicted to Love*, pp. 53–54.

95. Ibid., p. 54.

96. As quoted by Amy M. Spindler, "Patterns."

97. Elliott Smedley, "Escaping to Reality, Fashion Photographs in the 1990s," in *Fashion Cultures, Theories, Explorations and Analysis*, dir., Stella Bruzzi and Pamela Church Gibson, Routledge, New York, 2000, p. 153.

98. Peter Sloterdjik, *Selbstversuch. Ein Gespräch mit Carlos Oliveira*, C. Hanser Verlag, Munich, 1996.

99. As quoted by Amy M. Spindler, "The 90s Version of the Decadent Look," *New York Times*, May 7, 1996.

100. Ibid.

CHAPTER 4

101. As quoted by Françoise-Marie Santucci, *Kate Moss: Première biographie*, p. 118.

102. As quoted by Sheryl Garratt, "Million Dollar Baby," p. 305.

103. Ibid.

104. James Sherwood, "What Will Katie Do Next?" *The Independent*, August 2, 1998.

105. Angela McRobbie, "Fashion as a Culture Industry," in *Fashion Cultures*, (Bruzzi and Gibson, dir.) pp. 254–56.

106. Ibid.

107. As quoted by Sheryl Garratt, "Million Dollar Baby," p. 209.

108. Ibid., p. 209.

109. Roland Barthes, "The Face of Garbo," in *Mythologies*, selected and translated by Annette Lavers, Hill and Wang, New York, 1957, pp. 56–57.

110. Michel Foucault, "The Birth of Biopolitics," in *Michel Foucault, Ethics: Subjectivity and Truth*, edited by Paul Rabinow, The New Press, New York, 1997.

111. Michel Feher, "Self-Appreciation; or The Aspirations of Human Capital," *Public Culture*, Vol. 21, No. 1, Duke University Press, Durham, NC, 2009.

112. James Twitchell, *Branded Nation: The Marketing of Megachurch, College, Inc., and Museumworld*, Simon & Schuster, New York, 2004, p. 43.

113. Joseph Conrad, *Lord Jim*, Signet Classics, New York, 2009, p. 214.

114. Elfriede Jelinek, *Prinzessinnendramen: Der Tod und das Mädchen I–III und IV–V* [Princess Plays: Death and the Maiden I–III and IV–V], Berliner Taschenbuch Verlag, 2002.

115. Donna Haraway, "Race: Universal Donors in a Vampire Culture; It's All in the Family: Biological Kinship Categories in the Twentieth-Century United States," *The Haraway Reader*, Routledge, New York, 2004, Chapter 8, pp. 251–94.

116. Ibid.

117. Donna Haraway, "A Manifesto for Cyborgs: Science, Technology, and Socialist Feminism in the 1980s," *The Haraway Reader*, Chapter 1, pp. 7–46.

118. Donna Haraway, "Race…," *The Haraway Reader*, Chapter 8, p. 283.

119. Donna Haraway, "A Manifesto…," *The Haraway Reader*, Chapter 1, pp. 33–34.

120. Bruno Schulz, "Tailors' Dummies," in *The Street of Crocodiles*, from *The Complete Fiction of Bruno Schulz*, translated by Celina Wieniemska with an afterword by Jerzy Ficowski, Walker & Company, New York, 1989.

Photography Credits

KATE MOSS
THE MAKING OF AN ICON

▬▬▬▬▬

Original French title: *Kate Moss Machine*
Text copyright © Éditions La Découverte, 2010
Edition copyright © Éditions La Découverte, 2010

First edition in English, March 2012
Translation copyright © 2011 HarperCollins*Publishers*
Edition copyright © Harper Design,
An Imprint of HarperCollins*Publishers*

HarperCollins books may be purchased for educational, business, or sales promotional use. For information, please write: Special Markets Department, HarperCollins*Publishers,* 10 East 53rd Street, New York, NY 10022.

Published in 2012 by
Harper Design
An Imprint of HarperCollins*Publishers*
10 East 53rd Street
New York, NY 10022
Tel: (212) 207-7000
Fax: (212) 207-7654
harperdesign@harpercollins.com

Distributed throughout the world in the English language by
HarperCollins*Publishers*
10 East 53rd Street
New York, NY 10022
Fax: (212) 207-7654

ISBN: 978-0-06-202685-9

Library of Congress Control Number: 2011927592

Book Design by Agnieszka Stachowicz
Printed in China
First printing, 2012